THE FULLNESS of LIFE

Edited by Cedric W. Tilberg

Division for Mission in North America
Lutheran Church in America

Printed in U.S.A.

Library of Congress Catalog Card Number: 80-80740

ISBN: 0-936536-00-4

The drawing appearing on the cover, title page, and pages 25, 39, 63, 81, 103, 119, 135, 155, 175, & 191, titled *La Grandmere*, (B6327), is by Honore Daumier and is reproduced by permission of the National Gallery (Rosenwald Collection) in Washington, DC.

CONTENTS

Foreword

This book is written to help readers understand aging as an integral part of human development and to see all older adults as persons whose dignity is given by God. The volume is not designed as a handbook for congregational programs. Rather, it is intended to be a transmitter of information about the aging process and about the elderly. Little of the information presented is original with this book; it has been gleaned from many sources, as indicated in the references.

It is hoped that these pages will assist readers in dealing with their own aging and that of their friends and family members, and will stimulate this church to reflect a positive image of aging and the older adult in its worship, education, and fellowship, its institutional life and its advocacy for justice in society.

The book had its origin in the Consulting Committee on Aging, which served the Lutheran Church in America from 1974-1978. Early in 1976 members and staff persons began writing brief papers as bases for committee thinking and discussion. Even though many changes have taken place and other writers have participated, those papers were the nucleus of the present volume.

The following persons have been involved in the writing process; Tom Borzilleri, Martin J. Heinecken, Wade F. Hook, Paul G. Jacobson, Tamerra Moeller, Clifton L. Monk, Annie Ray Moore, Will C. Rasmussen, Murray H. Reich, Frederick J. Schumacher, and Cedric W. Tilberg.

Special appreciation is expressed to Dr. Tamerra Moeller, who has been on the faculty of the Institute of Gerontology of the University of Michigan and Wayne State University, and to Mr. Tom Borzilleri, Chief Economic Consultant for the National Retired Teachers Association/American Association of Retired Persons, for their invaluable assistance as both consultants and writers for the preparation of these chapters. Appreciation is also expressed to John Evenson and Fern Lee Hagedorn, Director and Assistant Director for Interpretation, Division for Mission in North America, who have helped guide the project at every stage. Useful criticism and support have come from other staff members of the Department for Church and Society.

Mrs. Judith Gross, Miss Mary Homan, Miss Dorothy Oscar, and Mrs. Carol Valenza spent many hours typing and proofreading manuscripts. They have also made many valuable suggestions.

The material in this book served as background for the social statement, "Aging and the Older Adult," which was adopted by the Ninth Biennial Convention of the Lutheran Church in America, July 12-19, 1978. The statement is printed as an appendix of this volume.

Cedric W. Tilberg, of the Department for Church and Society, served as staff coordinator of the Consulting Committee on Aging, drafter of the social statement, and editor of this book and author of several of its chapters. It is a privilege to offer this public expression of deep gratitude for Dr. Tilberg's wise and vigorous leadership in this critical area of the church's social ministry and public advocacy.

William H. Lazareth,
Director for Church and Society
Division for Mission in North America

Introduction

Charles Sylvester, 87 years old, is a trim man with a white goatee. He says he has never been very aware of moving into old age. For him retirement brought not a cessation of but a change in activities.

Someone asked Mr. Sylvester, what is the most important feature of getting older? He observed that some people talk about physical losses and others dwell upon the frequent disappearance of contemporaries, but neither is for him the essence of growing old. The crux for Mr. Sylvester is in answering the question, "Now that I have lived so long, what did my life really mean?" Although this question, in varying forms, has faced him all his life, today it is not a subject of mere intellectual speculation. It is critical, because the way he deals with it determines how he meets everything else—what remains to him of earthly life and death itself.

Herman Adler, aged 51, is a social worker. Mr. Adler tells about the early tension between his Jewish upbringing and the expectations of his neighborhood friends. As he moved through his teens his family and ethnic-religious heritage became increasingly important to him. One significant element was a deepening respect for older people, which was stimulated by the example of his father's admiration for the elders in his profession.

In his 40th year Mr. Adler became poignantly aware that there was more time behind him than might lie ahead. He had already discovered that he could no longer climb the tree in his backyard—his physical ability and stamina were not what they used to be. He had also faced the fact that he would never be President—his boyhood dreams were being replaced by a more realistic appraisal of himself. But, as he made his adjustment to middle age, he experienced a new acceptance of himself, a lessening of anxiety, and a fuller discovery of his family and ethnic background.

Mr. Adler, however, is conscious of losses in his life. He has watched the death of friends and loved ones in the generation ahead of him and is just starting to experience the death of a growing number of people in his own generation. As he looks to the future and ponders his own retirement and older years, he is concerned about the strength and variety of his human relationships, and he is worried that he has no avocations that interest him deeply—to a considerable degree his work is his life. He is glad that he has a capacity to enjoy being alone, that he has become flexible enough to be tolerant of people with life-styles different from his own, that he continues to be curious about "tomorrow," and that he likes facing the challenges of life.

Helen Sumter had lived an active life, characterized by deep involvement in her family and her church. Now 83 years old and fifteen years a widow, she has recently been forced by ill health and increasing disability to become a resident of Hope Manor, a proprietary nursing home. Because her funds are inadequate to pay for her care, she has applied for Medicaid. "I'm a pauper," she remarks with a mixture of wry humor and seriousness. Even though surrounded by activity and people, Mrs. Sumter is lonely. She is acutely aware of her new dependence upon others and realizes that this situation is likely to worsen with the passage of time. Her presence in the home relieves some of her anxiety about becoming a burden to her family. Nevertheless, she continues to fear, not so much death itself as the increasing physical helplessness and mental deterioration which sometimes accompany advancing age—and which she sees happening in many of her fellow residents. Although Mrs. Sumter has made several new friends in the home and the nurses are kind, the highlights of her week are visits from her son and his family and from her pastor. She wishes that more of her other friends from the church would come to see her, but she suggests that they are probably very busy.

Here are three people who are growing older. Their chronological ages are very different. Two are in old age, but Mrs. Sumter is an invalid and Mr. Sylvester is healthy and vigorous. Mr. Adler is middle-aged, but experiencing some of the crises that come with aging. Among these three there is much variety not only in age but in personality, life experience, present circumstances, and attitude toward growing older. They are typical of all of us.

The Aging Process

Aging is an inevitable part of being alive. We use the words "aging" and "old" during all stages of life. A child who comes of age is confirmed or pays full price for a movie. A young person comes of age for voting or driving a car. A major league baseball player is old at 35. At 65 or 70 a worker is deemed old enough to be retired.

The attitudes of society give meaning to adjectives such as "old." There is no inherent reason why we should not be as proud to be called "old" as to be called "young." Every period of life is important for human development and of significance to God, regardless of whether it is nearer the beginning or the end of our time on earth. But, in a society that exalts youth and undervalues the later years, people strive to act and appear "young." Perhaps we will arrive at a positive image of aging only when we can say with open self-assurance, "I am old."

By drawing lines between different life periods we create not one but several generation gaps. We then take the qualities associated with our ideal of youth and make them the measure for all age groups: ambition, drive, venturesomeness, physical vigor. This overemphasis upon the characteristics of youth often leads to disparagement of those associated with age.

A one-sided preoccupation with older people instead of young people would only compound the present error. Rather, we must take seriously the full span of life and see the meaning of each successive stage from birth to death in the context of all the years.

Biologists agree that almost as soon as the human organism stops growing the aging process begins, according to Robert C. Atchley, of the Scripps Foundation Gerontology Center, Miami University. Among the stages of life cited by Atchley, we will not dwell upon the first two, *childhood* and *adolescence,* since during those periods the organism is still growing. Although some signs of aging do occur in the 30's and 40's (*adulthood*), the questions with which we will deal in this book relate primarily to the three stages of advanced adulthood: *middle age* (40's and 50's), *later maturity* (60's and 70's) and *old age* (late 70's, 80's and 90's). The chronological ages are suggested merely as points of reference.

During *middle age* people become aware that they are aging. Certain physical and psychological changes are noticed. Chronic illness may appear. Children often "leave the nest" during this period, creating problems of adjustment for many parents. Attitudes toward work and career frequently undergo a transformation. People may start thinking about death as something they will meet face-to-face sooner or later.

Middle age is also a time for assessing one's life and, if necessary, revising one's goal for the future. As with Herman Adler, it can mean a lessening of anxiety and an awareness of new challenges in marriage or daily work.

During *later maturity* there is even greater awareness of the biological and sensory changes that accompany aging. Chronic health problems may limit activity and personal contacts. Retirement frequently reduces income and forces alteration in life- style. Movement of children and their families to more distant places, the death of friends and other contemporaries, and often the loss of a spouse will all exert significant influence upon persons in later maturity.

However, people more often than not learn to cope with these problems and reorient their lives. Their health and vigor, though less than in earlier years, are generally far better than is commonly recognized. With notable exceptions, large numbers of men and women are freer from responsibilities and social pressures. The result is that later maturity can be pleasant and productive for those who are willing and able to take advantage of it.

In *old age* persons naturally encounter increasing illness, frailty and disability. But there are great differences in the intensity with which these problems are experienced.

People cope during this period, too. They compensate for their losses and adjust to new situations. There is a tendency to review life and think more deeply about its meaning. If persons have come to this time with emotional maturity, then wisdom and understanding can grow.

Remember that at least two distinct stages are identified among persons beyond 60 or 65: later maturity and old age. These correspond roughly to Bernice Neugarten's distinction between "the young-old" and the "old-old." It is essential that we not fall into the common mistake of ascribing the characteristics of old age ("the old-old") to people who are in their later maturity ("the young-old"). The overwhelming majority of these "young-old" men and women are in relatively good health, and are mentally alert, able to learn, to make decisions of consequence and to share their wisdom with others. They do not fit at all the stereotypes of old age—infirm, dependent and incompetent. At the same time, we dare not fall into the opposite mistake of allowing our recognition of the vitality and potential of the "young-old" to prevent us from meeting the mounting needs of many of the "old-old."

Each of the stages of life from childhood through old age has its pluses and minuses, satisfactions and frustrations, triumphs and defeats, its purpose and significance. Each is a phase in the natural, normal unfolding of life as God has created it.

When we talk about aging, regardless of who we are, we are talking about ourselves and our total life. When we discuss older adults, the spotlight is again on ourselves. For all persons will be elderly — if they survive. Each, therefore, must struggle with the searching questions of how to live fully each stage of life and, ultimately, how to die.

Older Adults

Who Are They? How Many Are There?

Although aging can never be defined in terms of chronological age alone, census statistics use age 65 and over in giving demographic answers to the questions, who are the older adults? and how many are there? The U.S. Administration on Aging provides the following information, and the trends are similar in Canada:

* In 1977, one in every nine persons in the U.S. was 65+ (3.5 million men and women).
* The proportion of the population 65+ varied by race and ethnic origin: 11 percent of whites, 8 percent of blacks, and 4 percent of persons of Hispanic origin.

* During 1976, about 1.8 million persons reached the age of 65 and 1.2 million persons 65+ died, a net increase of 537,000 older Americans (1,470 per day).
* Between 1900 and 1977, the percentage of the U.S. population aged 65+ more than doubled (4.1 percent in 1900 to 10.9 percent in 1977) while the number increased over sevenfold (from 3 million to 23 million).
* At present death rates, the older population is expected to increase 35 percent to 32 million by the year 2000. If the present low birth rate persists, these 32 million will be 12.2 percent of the total population of about 260 million. If the birth rate should continue to decline, older adults would represent 12.9 percent of a total population of about 246 million.

It is obvious that we are talking about a sizable and important multitude of people. Indeed, men and women 65 and over are a significant part of the membership of the churches of North America, very likely constituting a percentage considerably higher than 10 percent.

What Are They Like?

Older adults are men and women who differ vastly from one another. One of the popular myths is that all the elderly are alike, that beyond a certain age they can be lumped in a mass. Nothing is further from fact. We actually become more *unlike* each other as we grow older. The oldest segment of the population displays greater variety than any other segment in personality traits, abilities and disabilities, social class and occupational background, religious and other serious interests, and what they like to do for fun. A lifetime of individual choices has determined the course any older adult has followed. As a matter of fact, all persons age in their own unique ways at their own unique rates. And within each one, different functions decline at different speeds. Some functions even seem to improve with age.

A Negative Image

Older adults have problems, often severe problems, and society does not have a good record of dealing with them. At least 15 percent of men and women 65 and over live "in poverty," as defined by the U.S. government, and their plight becomes increasingly desperate as inflation reduces the buying power of the dollars they have. Large numbers of older people occupy substandard housing, suffer from malnutrition and poor physical and mental health, and find it difficult to travel to necessary services, stores, family and friends, and places of worship, education and culture. But it may well be that the negative image of older adults and the aging process held by the general public, professional persons, the church, and many of the elderly themselves is the fundamental cause for concern.

There is much about aging that encourages a negative image. The medical, economic and social experiences that come with age must be faced realistically by both individuals and society. But an objective appraisal leads us to insist on the validity of other factors as well. If we are 65 or older, or if we think of ourselves at that age, we will be able to recognize the following as myths and stereotypes which demean older men and women:

* that their children usually have little contact with them;

* that they become more conservative with advancing years;
* that they are unable to learn and unwilling to accept anything new;
* that they lose interest in sexual expression after a certain age; and
* that large numbers of them become senile because of brain degeneration.

Myths and stereotypes like these influence the way younger people think about and behave toward the old.

Sharon Curtin, a young and angry American author, in her book *Nobody Ever Died of Old Age,* writes bitingly of the way in which we don't really see persons who are old. She tells about a scene she saw in a small park across from a nursing home one day. Young mothers and their children gathered at one side, and the older people from the home were on the other — "like so many pigeons perched on the benches." Every once in a while, when a youngster would happen to run over to the "wrong" side, the people would lean forward and smile. But before any communication could be established, the mother would murmur embarrassed apologies and take her child back to the "young" side. Miss Curtin observes that the children didn't seem to be afraid and the old people didn't seem to feel threatened. "The division of space was drawn by the mothers," who never really looked at the old men and women.

> These well-dressed young matrons had a way of *sliding* their eyes over, around, through the old people; they never looked at them directly. The old people might as well have been invisible; they had no reality for the youngsters, who were not

> permitted to speak to them, and they offended the aesthetic eye of the mothers.*

Expecting people to act in certain ways because they have reached a certain chronological age is a mistake. For example, expectations that may have some validity for the "old age" group may have no validity at all for those who have recently turned 65, yet we tend to apply the same expectations to them.

An important cause of a negative image of older adults is our deep fear of aging and death. This often influences the way medical doctors, nurses, social workers, pastors, young persons, and many others act toward those who are older. Since old people remind us of our own mortality, we hold them at arm's length.

As already mentioned, we are part of a culture which exalts, not young people themselves, but qualities ideally associated with youth, at the expense of those ideally associated with age.

Our society is committed to a work ethic, which puts a premium on achievement and productivity and regards a person's worth and identity as derived from work, particularly paid employment. This, obviously, is an ingredient in the negative image of the elderly.

There is a biological view of aging that assumes that the social problems of older persons are caused by their physical decline. Comparable weight should be given to psychological, spiritual and cultural forces and to the equally convincing hypothesis that our society's rejection of the old encourages and aggravates their physical and mental decline.

It is estimated that approximately 20 percent of older

*Sharon M. Curtin, *Nobody Ever Died of Old Age* (Boston: Little, Brown & Co. in association with the Atlantic Monthly Press, 1973), p. 34. Reprinted by permission.

persons require institutional care at some time during their later years, but only four percent are actually in institutions at any given time. The percentage is higher, naturally, among the "old age" group. Four percent of the older population is a large number of people, people to whose needs we should respond with the most sensitive understanding, but not nearly as large as the popular impression would have it. Another 8-10 percent, in addition, can continue living in their own homes or communities, if they receive supportive health, personal or social services. That still leaves a decisive majority of older adults who are quite capable of living active, productive and satisfying lives if society does not place obstacles in the way.

A negative image of aging leads us to believe men and women above a certain chronological age are less competent, less intelligent, less alert than they were before. Not only does this kind of image do immense damage to older adults themselves, causing emotional troubles, discouraging initiative, and fostering social and economic practices that discriminate against them; it also deprives us all of a fully-rounded appreciation of life. Maggie Kuhn, national convener of the Gray Panthers, quotes a young college student who was working with that organization: "The American youth cult hurts everybody. It robs the young people of a future and makes old age a tragedy. If you reach your peak at 25 and you are over the hill at 30, what do you have to look forward to for the next forty, fifty, or sixty years." Destructive attitudes toward aging deprive an entire society of the skills, labor, experience and wisdom of a significant portion of the population.

Dr. Robert N. Butler, director of the National Institute

of Aging, coined the term "Ageism." He defines ageism as "a deep and profound prejudice against the elderly which is found to some degree in all of us." The church and society have no more basic task in relation to older adults than to correct the negative image and root out ageism.

Other Problems of Older Adults

The 1971 White House Conference on Aging identified nine major areas of concern:

income

employment and retirement

physical and mental health

housing

nutrition

transportation

retirement roles and activities

education

spiritual well-being

The reader may think of other areas of concern that deserve to be in this list. Indeed, the 1981 White House Conference on Aging is likely to draw up a somewhat different catalogue.

The conviction expressed in this book is that even the most severe problems in these areas of concern will be dealt with most effectively within the context of a positive rather than a negative image of aging and the older adult. The change called for by this statement is *radical.* It involves a transformation in the basic concepts, attitudes and values which determine how our society orders its life, recognizes the dignity and worth of individuals, and assigns roles to people of every age.

In the task of changing fundamental attitudes older persons themselves carry a primary but by no means exclusive responsibility. The ways they view life, human values, the aging process, persons of every generation, and their own place in church and community will be highly influential. The rapidly growing numbers of older men and women, coupled with their improving educational status and increasing assertiveness, can be a powerful force in the eventual elimination of ageism. Certainly the church is in a unique position to witness to the oneness of all persons, regardless of age (and sex, race, ethnic origin, economic status), as created in the image of God, and to draw out the implications of this witness in every facet of its own life and that of society.

Within the context of a radical change in basic attitudes, the solutions to the kind of problems cited by the White House Conferences require commitment and priority effort by government at all levels, and by other social institutions. This is not likely to happen without commitment and priority effort by the citizens who choose the decision makers and support and monitor their actions, including everyone who reads these words. The solutions also call for effective action by community organizations, social service and educational agencies and institutions, churches, synagogues and other religious organizations, families, and older adults themselves.

In connection with some of these areas of concern, the church's most important task may be to advocate public policy that advances justice for the elderly, especially those who are most vulnerable. This is true both because massive problems require the massive resources possessed only by government, and also because the primary responsibility for dealing with some problems, such as income maintenance, belongs to the whole society, not just a part of it.

With regard to some other areas of concern, however, the church has responsibility for more direct action — through its congregations and synods, its agencies and institutions. The fostering of good mental health, at least in the preventive sense; pre-retirement planning; constructive retirement roles and activities; encouragement of and guidance for better nutrition; lifelong education that enriches living; spiritual well-being — these are all areas in which the church in its various expressions has a role to play. Some regional church judicatories have trained volunteers, often older persons, to give leadership to congregations and clusters of congregations in meeting these concerns. In some cases, church social service agencies and institutions are using their expertise to assist in parish ministries with older adults.

Many projects that enable older adults to function more effectively in everyday life — transportation, chore services, home health care, day care, senior centers — are best carried out as community enterprises. Alert congregations can demonstrate how to set up such projects and spin them off when the larger community is ready to take hold. Some programs, of course, regardless of community involvement, are always appropriate activities of the congregation as a caring fellowship. Examples are visiting, telephone reassurance, and "informal" (as contrasted with professional, agency-sponsored) homemaker service. Indeed, the church's active, competent engagement in various forms of service to older persons, whether in the informal or the professional sense, strengthens its ability to be an influential advocate for justice as it works with communities and with agencies of government.

Following these words concerning service, however, one more emphatic word must be spoken, reiterating that the most important "service" to older adults is to remove all social barriers to their participation and leadership in church and community. Even those whose potential for active life has become limited must be cared for in full respect for their significance as persons created in God's image.

Older men and women, let it be remembered, are simply people — people who happen to have lived longer than some others.

I

Older Adults in Society

Older Adults in Society

A basic sociological perspective is that a person's self-image and self-esteem depend upon responses from other people. The individual discovers selfhood in the process of social interrelationships. Through the attitudes of others each person learns to "see" and to evaluate her or his own appearance, feelings, and behavior. We gain a feeling about ourselves by imagining what others think about the way we look and act. Without this "social mirror," there is no sense of self.

As we apply this theory to the later years, we find that many of the elderly have a low opinion of themselves. The attitudes, gestures, and speech addressed to older persons are often filled with pity, derogation, condescension and varying degrees of patronizing treatment. The result is the gradual destruction of individuality and dignity. The elderly become enslaved to the broad generalizations and myths of their own inferiority. To nourish and perpetuate such misconceptions contributes unnecessarily to the anxieties and extra stress of aging.

The truth is that aging is normal, universal, and variable. Every person ages and copes with aging in a unique way. Careful research indicates that the rates of physiological, psychological, and social aging differ greatly within the human being and from person to person. These findings refute the notion that the old are unproductive, inflexible, and withdrawn from life.

There has always been a certain ambivalence about age, in both classical literature and public attitudes. The dichotomies include generous/miserly, good/bad, serene/disquieted, saints/sinners. In analyzing societal attitudes toward old age, W. Andrew Achenbaum, in *Old Age Dependency in America Since 1777,* identifies four historical periods in American history:

1775-1865, veneration;
1865-1914, obsolescence;
1914-1940, stronger notions of obsolescence and perception of old age as a "national" problem; and
1940-the present, continued institutionalization of dependency of the aging, and development of a national bureaucratic structure to deal with the problem.

Older Adults in the Family and the Work Force

Ours is becoming an aging population; and Americans, partly because of the impact of that fact, are again revising their ideas about aging. Many sociological factors significantly affect the makeup of the elderly household:

* Most persons 65 and over live in family settings.
* Most older men are married (77 percent); most older women are widowed (52 percent).
* There are more than five widows for every widower in the population 65 and over.

* Approximately one million or 4 percent of all older persons reside in institutions of all kinds at any given time.
* Eighty-eight percent of the residents of nursing and personal care homes are 65 and over. Approximately one-sixth of them are confined to bed at all times, and another one-fourth are bedfast for part of the time.
* In the non-institutional population, the numbers of older men and women living in family settings are about the same (7.6 million men, 7.5 million women), but, since there are many more older women than older men (146 per 100), the proportion of older men in family settings is 83 percent, and of women, 58 percent.
* Among older people the proportion living in family settings decreases rapidly with advancing age.
* More than one-third of all older persons live alone or with non-relatives (42 percent of older women, 17 percent of older men).
* Fourteen percent of the older population are in the labor force.

The Family As The Group of All Groups

The twentieth century has brought dramatic change in family social organization and structure. Among the changes reported are smaller numbers of children, progressive liberalization of views toward marriage and sex roles, increased diversity between older and younger generations in life-styles, increased mobility of children, and reduced parent-child interdependence. Ours has been called the age of the fragile family, the family in transition. All of these changes have had important implications for older persons.

The family is the major source of help and protection in old age. On the other side of the coin, family relationships can contribute significantly to negative aspects of aging. The way middle-aged and older family members deal with their own aging profoundly influences the way younger members deal with the aging process in their lives. The attitudes of the middle-aged toward their parents go far to determine how their children feel and behave toward all the generations ahead of them. The image of aging held within the family circle is likely to be a stronger force than the attitudes of the community in raising or lowering the self-esteem and self-confidence of the elderly.

Research studies are revealing some encouraging data about contacts today among family members who do not live under one roof. Ethel Shanas, a professor of sociology at the University of Illinois, reports on a study of a sample of the three-fourths of the elderly in private households who have living children. The great majority live close enough to an adult child to call on him or her for help if it is needed. More than 80 percent see one of their children as often as once a week. They tend to have more interaction with daughters and their families than with sons and their families. Of approximately three-fourths of older adults with living siblings, three out of ten men and four out of ten women see a sibling during a one-week period.

In a research project conducted twenty years ago at Duke University, 161 persons 60 and over, living in the vicinity of Durham, North Carolina, were intensively interviewed. Asked, "Do you think your family or close relatives neglect you?" 81 percent responded, "Not at all," while only 19 percent answered, "completely" or "a little."

These findings do not support conventional generalizations about family rejection and social isolation of older adults. It is more difficult, of course, to document the quality of the contacts and interaction indicated by these studies.

Most older people with living spouses tend to see their marriages in a positive light, and many report improvement and increased satisfaction in the later stages. Expressiveness and companionship are among the most rewarding aspects of marriage at older ages. The most troublesome aspects are different values and philosophies of life and lack of mutual interests. Others point out that sex roles which are less rigid and an increase in equality of the partners in the relationship contribute to the happiness of the older couple.

But the endings are not all happy. Studies of marriage adjustment in later years show that women with husbands retired five or more years are more likely to wish the men had started retirement later than are wives of more recently retired men. In 1975, 3.3 percent of people 65-74 years of age were divorced; and in the same year, of those 75 years of age and older, 1.5 percent were divorced (Statistical Abstract of the U.S.). It has been suggested that more of those who reach old age without ever marrying may be expected to experience severe loneliness. Those who married more than once may have strained relations with former partners and with their children by former marriages. However, they may be better off than someone with a lasting but uncongenial marriage.

Trauma, guilt feelings, and family crises often accompany the entry of many elderly persons into nursing homes. For a number of these persons, there is no other means of providing personal and nursing care; and many of these care facilities are part of the ministry of the church, with humanistic and Christian policies and staff members. Many, also, have come under journalistic attack and government investigation. A key issue to keep in mind at all times is the right of personal decision-making on the part of those older persons capable and desirous of exercising this freedom. Too often, bureaucratic policies dictate schedules, room assignments, visiting hours, and access to special services when needed. Medical bureaucracies and administrative actions in some cases devastate freedom of choice at the time of terminal illness and death.

Physical incapacities, genetic traits, and medical problems of the aging can be modified only within certain limits. The most optimistic outlook for improving the quality of life for the elderly and guaranteeing their right to personal choice rests upon the sociological variable — that is, in changing the attitudes and behavior of those persons most intimately and most constantly involved in their lives (children, other relatives, and friends).

Mandatory Retirement

Winston Churchill at 62 was a failure. He had been, at times, a significant figure in more than one political party, but now he was out of both parties. Three years later he was called on to become Prime Minister and to save his country in time of war; and he did it. Again, at the age of 78 he was Prime Minister of Great Britain. Arthur Fiedler directed the Boston Pops Orchestra into his mid-eighties. Andres Segovia, famous classical guitarist, made a tour of the United States at the age of 83. Rose Kennedy, now nearly 90, has remarkably survived extreme grief and tragedy. Albert Schweitzer won the Nobel Peace Prize for his work as a humanitarian at the age of 77, and he continued to work at a missionary hospital in Equatorial Africa until his death at the age of 90.

The Bible assumes work to be the natural activity of man. "Man goes forth to his work and to his labor until the evening," says the writer of Psalm 104. The basic assumption of the biblical viewpoint is that work is a part of the divinely ordered structure of the world and human nature. "It is through man's work that he knows himself to be a human being. Animals do not work; they obey their instincts; they make no resolves, no plans; to be able to do these things is the great and dangerous privilege of man,"* writes Emil Brunner. Sociological arguments, as well as those based upon a biblical understanding of man, support the recent U.S. governmental act lifting the minimum mandatory retirement age in private industry from 65 to 70.

Work, at any age, gives shape and content to human existence; it is a basic activity in which we assert and express our humanity. It binds us to reality.

In American society, we are socialized and conditioned to derive our sense of identity primarily from work (jobs and professional status). For the same society, which bestows meaning and recognition chiefly through the consequence of one's work, to institutionalize and to demand forced retirement and involuntary unemployment for workers with the ability and desire to continue to work is highly questionable.

Human beings seek the accomplishment of concrete, objective ends. Because in our humanity we are such

*Emil Brunner, *The Divine Imperative* (Philadelphia: The Westminster Press, 1936), p. 385, © 1947 by W. L. Jenkins. Reprinted by permission of publisher.

agents, we are possessed of an inclination for effective work and a distaste for futile effort. Using a sociological perspective, the case against mandatory retirement is based in part upon the following findings/assertions:

* Mandatory retirement at a specified chronological age, in the words of Geneva Mathiasen, "makes no allowances for individual differences and goes counter to the basic tenet of democracy which upholds the right of every man to the full development and the exercise of his inherent abilities."
* Forced withdrawal from work for many persons is a threatening, alienating experience; it generates a feeling and self-definition of incompetence whereby one no longer considers himself or herself competent to function as a free human being.
* The American Medical Association Committee on Aging states that there is ample clinical evidence that physical and emotional problems can be brought on or made worse by denial of employment opportunities. Enforced idleness may even be characterized as a disease-producing or disability-producing condition.
* A 1974 Harris Poll revealed that nearly 40 percent of the 20 million Americans retired at the time that the poll was taken would prefer to be actively engaged in work that would allow them to contribute to the mainstream of American society.
* A 1975 Harris Poll conducted for the National Council on the Aging revealed that 86 percent of those over 65 responded affirmatively to the statement, "Nobody should be forced to retire because of age if he wants to continue working and still is able to do a good job."
* According to Harvey Shapiro, employees from 65 to

70, and even up to 75, generally perform as well as younger workers in jobs not requiring heavy physical labor. While younger workers usually have more education and learn more rapidly, older employees are more likely to display better judgment and stable work habits.

* Enforced replacement of workers on the basis of some standardized timetable could slow the rate of scientific and social progress. Concentration and prolongation are necessary for the human effort.

Social Pathologies

No sociologist would deny that there are serious problems related to aging. In an early sociological classic Emile Durkheim points out that older people commit suicide more frequently than younger ones. The 65 and over category represents 10 percent of the population, but it has 25 percent of the suicides. White males over 65 have three times the rate for 20-24 year old females. Furthermore, 85 percent of suicides over 60 have active serious physical illness at the time of death (Statistical Abstract of the U. S.). According to Uniform Crime Reports, out of a total of 16,605 murder victims in the United States in 1976, 1,084 were 65 and over.

One writer, Jeremy Main, says that the elderly are among our society's habitual economic victims. Almost 16 percent of persons 65 and older are below poverty level. Among adults, poverty occurs with much greater frequency for the elderly than for the non-elderly. On the average, the elderly must live on approximately half the income of the non-elderly. Studies have indicated that the elderly themselves have determined that they need one-third more than the income which they have. Typically, the income which they estimated as necessary during retirement amounted to two-thirds of their pre-retirement income. To use the "near-poor" standard would significantly increase the number of people on an inadequate income. Conservative estimates suggest that 20 percent of older Americans are poor. They are frequently the victims of unscrupulous insurance salesmen, repairmen, hearing aid vendors, real estate salesmen, and nursing home operators.

The aged are considerably more likely to be functionally illiterate than people under the age of 65. Furthermore, as D. Warner Schaie, of the University of Southern California, observes, the real intellectual problem for older people is the fact that, although they are functioning at the level they attained in their younger days, this level is often no longer appropriate for successful performance in contemporary society.

Approximately 10 percent of alcoholics in treatment are age 60 or over while 3 percent of drug abusers are age 50 or over. The elderly alcoholic group has a higher proportion of men, Caucasians, and individuals with a lower educational level. Most elderly alcoholics began abusing alcohol in their 40's; the older alcoholic is more likely to drink daily than the younger alcoholic; and the older alcoholics are more likely to complete treatment than their younger counterparts.

A further problem is that of "status-role." All older persons inevitably face the problem of social loss—losing such roles as co-worker, colleague, committee or board member, fellow member of voluntary organizations and associations, and numerous parenthood functions. Deep losses occur as friends, spouses, and other family members die. One member of a senior citizens' center began her fourth car pool after all her former riders had died. The most intense shock during life for most persons is the death of a spouse. It is often difficult to compensate for these losses of roles and relationships.

There is no question that the elderly often have a difficult position in American life and that the problems and pathologies will not readily go away. There is growing evidence and support in the late 1970's, however, for accepting older people as vital human beings and for stressing their normal capacities for self-direction, learning and adjustment. In spite of the profile presented here, older people are better educated, healthier, and have more income than ever before; are more articulate than ever and show a higher level of political consciousness; are maintaining memberships in voluntary associations; and are more aggressive in demanding change.

Conclusion

New priorities which put the meaning of aging in proper human perspective are needed. In tackling the complex issues related to aging, the policy makers of society need the assistance, not only of medical and legal scholars, economists, and sociologists, but also of the theologian and the churchman with a strong biblical thrust. The church can lead the way in infusing into contemporary culture a new attitude toward aging, one which stresses creative potential rather than obsolescence.

"What should a society be in order that in his last years a man might still be a man?" asks Simone de Beauvoir in *The Coming of Age.* It must be a social aggregate that proclaims voluntarism and freedom of choice as enduring human values; one in which age is irrelevant; and one which shows as much concern for the views and welfare of older people as it does for the rights and needs of any other group. It would be immoral to lose this vision.

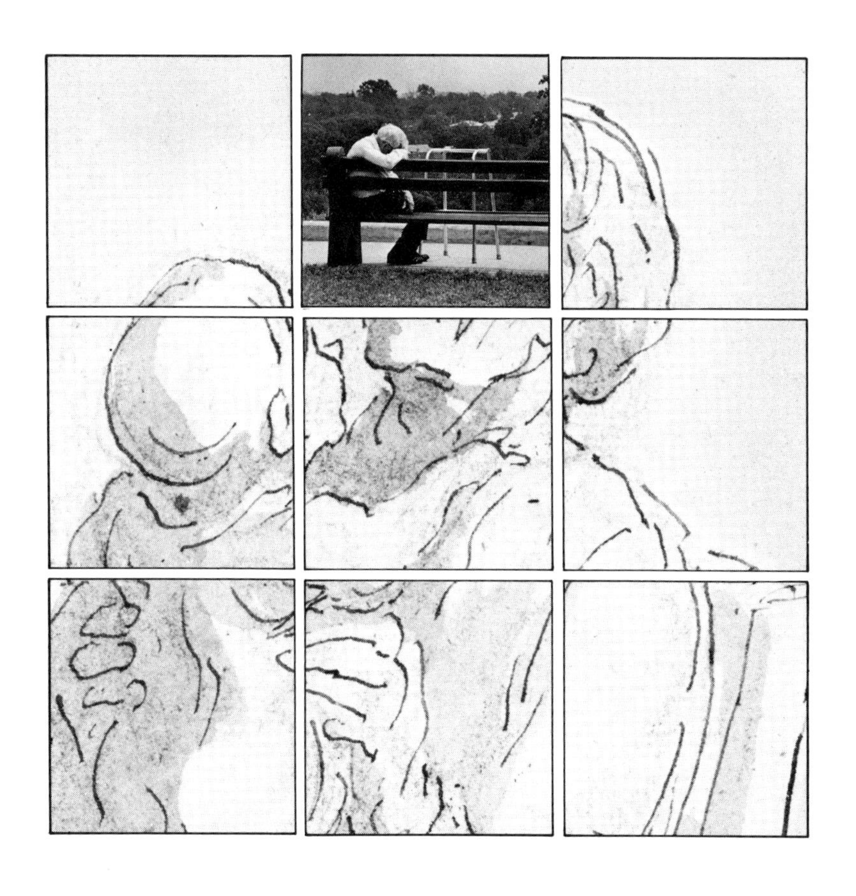

2 The Psychology of Aging

The Psychology of Aging

Mental Functioning

Memory

"Am I losing my mind? I forget the names of people to whom I was introduced yesterday. I even have difficulty remembering facts that I had mastered years ago. My granddaughter can run rings around me in learning newfangled ways of doing things. I feel so embarrassed when I forget the names of friends I have known for years. What's wrong with me? Am I losing my mind?"

No, it is quite unlikely that this worried person is losing his or her mind. Ask yourself how well you learned names twenty-five years ago. And how long ago, really, did you begin to forget those important facts you learned in school when you were young? It has been observed that a young person forgetting is called "absent-minded" but an old person forgetting is "senile." Older people's sense of competence may be adversely affected by changes in memory. Although these changes are common in the later years, to each individual they can seem unique and, at times, troubling. Even though persons may have difficulty remembering dates, medical instructions and names, this is a far different thing from losing their minds. They may still have a good command of language, the ability to solve problems, and likely, more information on many topics than younger persons.

Individuals should learn to be tolerant of themselves. Degrading comments like "I'm so stupid," only undermine one's sense of competence. It is also important to know, and to tell friends and relatives, that when one is feeling tired, ill, or "under fire," memory may falter.

Here are some memory aids that some older women and men find useful:

* a large, plainly visible wall calendar for recording appointments;
* a pad of paper and a pencil for writing down information, e.g. a doctor's instructions;
* a conscious effort to associate the names of new acquaintances with their faces, clothes, interests, and mutual friends;
* repetition of new names out loud in addition to writing them down; and
* exercise of the memory.

People should assist each other. They should give their names clearly and help finish introductions (but not too quickly) if friends introducing them show signs of forgetting. A person who is known to have difficulty recalling the events of last week should be encouraged to talk about what he or she does remember. Sharing memories from early years can be rewarding and helpful.

The Ability to Reason

According to the best research, the aging process by itself does not reduce reasoning ability. Misunderstanding has arisen from the performance of older adults in traditional IQ tests, which showed a decline in intelligence after the 20's. Such testing has been cross-sectional. This means that it is applied to a broad sample of people at a given time, without taking into consideration the different educational and other life experiences that have brought them to this point. Older adults by and large have had less formal education than younger people, and this is bound to affect their performance in "intelligence" tests. Instruments are now being devised that will examine independence level, the fruits of experience, adaptability, and the ability to make decisions, solve problems, and cope with stress.

Studies of the same persons tested over a period of years reveal that older adults can retain the ability to learn throughout their lives, provided they continue to put that ability to work and allow themselves time to organize and assimilate what they learn. Thus education, both as retraining for new jobs or new careers and as enrichment of life, is as appropriate for the elderly as for the young. A white-haired man in his mid-80's began the study of Persian. When asked "Why are you doing this at your age?", he answered simply, "I'll never be younger." Older adults who have been creative in earlier years do not lose this capacity merely because of added years. Indeed, there have been many instances of creativity increasing with age.

Personality

Another significant factor influencing a person's sense of competence and adjustment to growing old is personality — the individual's characteristic way of understanding and dealing with life. Despite basic continuity, old age is not merely an extension of middle age. It is a definite stage of life with its own challenges and rewards. It calls for the willingness to admit limitations, change physical activities and social roles, find new ways to fulfill one's needs, develop new criteria for self-evaluation, and establish new values and goals for one's life. These are tasks that face all older people.

The way in which persons perform these tasks in the later years usually reflects the personality patterns manifested in the middle years. Some individuals are able to make the necessary decisions and adopt a constructive and resilient style of life. Some avoid fundamental decisions, either because they are afraid to let go of the drives and directions of middle age, or because they want to withdraw from people, responsibilities and problems. Still others are passive and dependent, apathetic, disorganized, or willing to let others make decisions.

Since personality styles in the older years are believed to have continuity with those of the earlier years, chronological age is not a decisive factor in adjusting to growing old. Far more influential factors are health, financial resources, social and cultural environment, work/activity situations, marital status, family and friendship relationships, and the attitudes of society, especially of younger and middle-aged people, toward older adults. In interacting with such forces the man or woman adjusts to aging.

The Psychological Effects of Sensory Changes

It is very important to distinguish between disease and the natural changes that belong to aging. As we grow older we experience bodily changes, such as a possible decline in various sensory processes — but these are not disease. Even many physicians fail to make this distinction and thus give the impression that aging itself is a disease. Let's look at some of the changes that affect the senses.

Sight

The two most vital senses are seeing and hearing. Multiple changes may occur in the functioning of both senses, affecting performance of many daily tasks. Small items, such as newspaper print, labels on cans and instructions accompanying many products, are seen less accurately than may be desirable or safe. Also the older person often needs greater illumination to see objects as clearly as someone who is younger, and blue and green objects of any size may be more difficult to distinguish than those colored red, orange or yellow. Glare may become a serious problem and, in addition, an older man or woman may find it harder to adapt to darkness, as when walking into a motion picture theater or driving the car at night.

The knowledge we have about glare and color changes can be used to make practical adjustments in the environment. To decrease glare, diffused lighting is best. If there is one bright lamp in a room, an overhead light can help reduce the glare caused by the lamp. Sheer curtains across a window can also cut down glare without significantly darkening the room. Also, local grocers and pharmacists should be informed about glare, so that they will avoid white-backed labels and signs and use larger print in a color that contrasts with the background.

In addition to reducing the effects of glare, the older person and others should be aware of ways to decrease accidents caused by a lack of contrasting colors. One of the most useful aids is a roll of heavy colored tape. Wherever there is a flight of steps or a change in elevation in the floor, a strip of tape contrasting sharply with the color of the floor should be placed at the point of junction. This kind of tape should also be placed on glass doors, on the dials of stoves to indicate the "OFF" position, and on shower controls to designate the "LUKEWARM" position. Furthermore, spills and other accidents can be decreased if cups, glasses and plates have clearly marked rims. In general, strongly contrasting colors should be used to identify potentially dangerous areas both indoors and outside. Also, the colors of walls, rugs, curtains and furniture should be chosen with this consideration in mind.

Hearing

Approximately one-third of the population over 65 has hearing and understanding problems. Older people have difficulty hearing the more high-pitched tones. They often fail to comprehend because of poor enunciation, rapid speech, or background noises such as conversations, televisions, air conditioners or traffic. Hard-of-hearing persons frequently have difficulty with telephone conversations, public speeches, classes, group gatherings, and interaction with children.

Speaking slowly and distinctly, using lower tones, facing the older person, and catching his or her attention before speaking are much more effective than talking loudly. Hearing aids should be purchased only from firms that are well known for competence and integrity. Older adults often dislike hearing aids, and adjustment to an aid may be trying and discouraging. It is important for all concerned to be patient during this period of adaptation.

It should be recognized that hearing losses may cause considerable social isolation. Anyone who finds it hard to follow a conversation, even among a group of friends or family members, is likely to feel isolated. Even a moderate hearing loss may be accompanied by misunderstandings and feelings of suspicion and distrust. Older people with this handicap may try to "fill in" what they think someone else has said. They often begin to fear the worst.

Hard-of-hearing individuals should not hesitate to request that a situation be changed so that it will facilitate their hearing.

Other Senses

Changes may also take place in the other senses. The senses of taste and smell do not usually decline to a noticeable extent until individuals are in their late 70's. It is thought that older people have less sensitivity to pain than do younger people, but this is still uncertain. Also, the weakening of the sense of balance with the consequent danger of falling is frequently a problem of the later years.

Processing of Sensory Information

Older adults process sensory information with less speed than those who are younger. This has nothing to do with intelligence. Our speaking more slowly and being careful not to jump quickly from one subject to another can significantly improve the older person's comprehension. Allowing her or him time to assimilate information and to respond fully is also helpful.

Dealing with Sensory Handicaps

The general public must become more alert to the effect sensory losses can have on the elderly, often causing isolation, irritability and depression. In fact, sometimes this condition is identified with mental impairment—a tragic error. But it is just as essential for those who are suffering sensory deprivation to learn how to deal with their problems constructively. They must become more candid about their handicaps and more assertive in asking people to speak both slowly and clearly or to turn on more than one light in a room so as to reduce glare. Every church—and every other public building—should be evaluated and changed where necessary to assure easy access and free mobility for infirm and handicapped persons, large numbers of whom are elderly.

Toward a Broader View of Sexuality

Human beings are capable of sexual activity into their 70's, 80's and beyond. Changes take place in the realm of sexuality, but these changes do not follow the common stereotypes. There may be a "slowing down" in both sexes, and there are other physiological problems, most of which can be treated. Even prostate surgery in men and menopause in women have negative effects upon the continued enjoyment of sexuality far less often than is commonly assumed, particularly if there is opportunity to receive accurate information. Societal attitudes, which are shared by older people themselves, are more decisive than physiological conditions in reducing activity in later life. For example, an epithet like "dirty old man" reveals a demeaning image, implying that beyond a certain age it is not possible, or even proper, for men and women to engage in sexual relations. This and other socio-psychological factors are enough to discourage many people. These attitudes also have had an unfortunate influence upon many homes for the elderly, which, by making it difficult for their residents to find privacy and to establish personal relationships of their own choosing, have failed to affirm the sexuality of older adults.

Each person needs to relate to others in terms of her or his sexuality, with a "glance, touch, smile, a friendly word, a kiss, or an embrace," says Nancy E. Hinkley, adult education specialist from Raleigh, North Carolina. Dr. Hinkley points out that most studies have dealt with the physical aspects of the sex act. While this information is useful, more is needed regarding the deep longing for affection and its natural forms of expression. We should see the totality of the sexual needs of the older man or woman as he or she comes to the fulfillment of the life cycle and to the full acceptance of one's aging self. A widow in her 80's said plaintively, "It is at least ten years since any of my family has really touched me."Although her family must be more alert to the importance of her cry, this woman herself has some responsibility to take initiative, to reach out toward them and others in such a way as to encourage contact. The result can be an experience of mutual affection that warms hearts and resolves tensions.

The existence of myths and wrong information may be due in part to memories of the not-too-distant past when life expectancy was 47 years and those who lived beyond that age were often not healthy enough to be sexually active. The book, *Sex After Sixty*, by Robert Butler and Myrna Lewis, contains much information of personal importance to individuals in understanding sexual development and needs in later life. It stresses that many older people choose to enjoy a satisfying life without physical sex and that each person is entitled to live in a way that he or she finds most fulfilling.

Adjustment to Physical Changes

Along with natural changes in sensory processes and sexuality the older person becomes aware of declines in physical strength, reserve capacity, resilience, and a sense of health. The declines can have an adverse effect upon self-esteem and morale. A man or woman may be tempted to withdraw from association with people because of a feeling of inadequacy or rejection. He or she may hesitate to undertake otherwise desirable activities for fear of accident or illness. Sometimes an annoying mannerism or changed appearance caused by disease will lead others to stigmatize and avoid the person affected. It is essential that competent counseling and friendly group activity help older adults who are troubled in these ways to "come out of their shells" and participate as fully as possible in human fellowship. Also, vigorous exercise and good nutrition, under competent medical guidance, can improve heart action, lung capacity, mental well-being and relaxation.

Nevertheless, the older person must develop a mature, confident attitude toward the changes which are part of normal aging. Such an attitude will receive indispensable support from improvement in society's respect for age, acceptance by the family and the community, demonstrations of affection, and sensitive human communication.

Coping with Mental and Emotional Disturbances

Mental and emotional disturbances among older adults are often misunderstood. Occasional emotional distress is common to large numbers of people of all ages; it should not be identified as mental illness unless it leads to serious behavioral disorders which attract the attention of family and friends or even of law enforcement people and other professional personnel. Very frequently, these problems stem from cultural and environmental causes as well as physical and psychological changes.

Mental disorders may include anxiety, depression, hypochondria, paranoia, and suicidal tendencies. Depression, for example, manifests itself in such symptoms as boredom, short attention span, inability to make decisions, fatigue, bodily malfunctions, sleep disturbance, and feelings of guilt and self-pity. Depression can often be treated. The patient, especially if he or she is older, needs the care of a medical doctor, along with someone trained in mental health, such as a social worker, psychologist or psychiatrist.

Pastors and congregations may assist persons suffering from depression, not only by helping them secure professional treatment but also by assuring them that such emotional problems are not the result of loss of faith or the judgment of God. Since they may stem from a variety of causes, they are the experience of believers and nonbelievers alike.

Another class of mental disorders among old people is organic brain syndromes, which are impairments caused by deterioration of the brain tissue. *Reversible brain syndromes* are brought about by assaults on the brain, such as strokes, alcoholism, infection, malnutrition, and injuries. Since these can often be successfully treated, it is essential that the patient be taken as quickly as possible to a physician and/or hospital. *Chronic brain syndromes* are irreversible, eventually fatal, processes of mental deterioration which usually go by the term "senility." It is not easy to distinguish between these conditions and those which are reversible. In any case, the most competent medical care is required. Even if such diseases cannot be cured, many of the physical and emotional problems that go with them can be successfully treated, so that the person improves in his or her functioning.

It is extremely important for families and close friends to be patient and understanding of those experiencing mental or emotional disturbance. Adults and children tend to become frightened or uncomfortable if the older man or woman does not seem to recognize them. Every effort must be made, nevertheless, to communicate with sensitivity. Tell him or her who you are, who she or he is, and where you both are. Share memories. Do not be discouraged if there is no discernible response. And remember: the loving touch of hands, hugging and kissing may mean far more than an exchange of words. Even persons in deep comas have often shown improved heart performance when their hands were held by doctors or nurses.

Emotional Problems of Retirement

A person's attitude toward retirement, indeed one's attitude toward becoming older, will go far in determining how he or she will adjust to retirement. The individual who has derived great satisfaction and identity from a job may find it difficult to deal with a long period of unemployment. If a man or woman resents being forced out, this resentment may be a problem in itself. The fact is that many people with a positive orientation toward work have made excellent adjustments to retirement. Some who have spent their careers in routine and uninteresting jobs may be relieved by the change. They may look forward either to leisure or to the opportunity to launch second careers, whether in paid employment or volunteer activity.

Retirement is feared when there is not enough income, a prospect made even worse by the continually rising rate of inflation. Women will likely face this problem more than men simply because women have usually worked for lower pay and because they usually live longer. Concerns about retirement income will not only influence the time they retire, if they have a choice; it will have much to do with the activities in which they engage after they retire. They may try to keep on working at some job as long as possible in order to support themselves and their families. This will be advantageous especially if the Social Security retirement test, which places a ceiling on earnings before benefits are limited, is modified or eliminated.

The psychological adjustment of older men and women to retirement will be assisted greatly if the emphasis is upon the *right* of those who have contributed to a nation's prosperity to be supported in their later years, rather than upon the shaky assumption that older workers are no longer capable of doing their jobs. Because nearly everyone today experiences retirement, the experience is becoming socially more acceptable. Furthermore, it appears that the "work ethic" is losing its force. Factors like these are important in fostering a positive view of retirement.

Finally, it has been demonstrated that effective programs of preparation for retirement assist older adults in making the transition. Such programs, however, now cover at most about ten percent of the labor force, and few of them reach workers early enough to be of maximum value. Even if no organized program is available, it will be to the advantage of anyone, in cooperation with his or her spouse if married, to make as specific plans as possible years ahead of the retirement date, not only in financial matters but in such areas as location and housing, activities, and personal relationships.

Losses and Gains

In addition to natural bodily changes and vulnerability to disease, the aging process usually brings with it other experiences which have profound influence on the later years.

There are many possible losses: loss of job through retirement; loss of role as breadwinner or homemaker or parent; loss of finances; loss of status, prestige, independence or mobility; loss of spouse, children, family members, and friends; loss of opportunity for sexual expression; loss of parts of the body through surgery; loss of a familiar home, neighborhood, or cherished possessions.

All losses involve in some degree the kind of grief process that is characteristic of both dying and bereavement. Dr. Elisabeth Kübler-Ross suggests that the following steps are part of that process: *denial* (of loss, illness) *anger* (focused on self, the person who has died, the doctor, God, the pastor), *bargaining* ("If I do this,...," "If only I had done that...."), *depression* (sense of loss and loneliness, and *acceptance* (not the same as a discouraged resignation to your fate). Depending upon the severity of loss, it is necessary to work through some or all of these steps.

There are gains, too, as people grow older: freedom from the routine and rigors of a job; opportunity to launch new activities; freedom to be more selective in choosing friends and to build personal relationships for their own sake, rather than for the sake of improving one's success at work or in the community social structure; freedom to advocate causes in which one believes without fear of reprisal. Maggie Kuhn says, "We old people can speak out for justice — we have nothing to lose!"

Bereavement and Loneliness

Bereavement is a nearly universal human experience, but that does not make it less painful. Whether it involves the death of husband or wife, parent, child or sibling, another family member or a close friend, the bereaved person usually has to live through most or all of the basic steps of grief that Kübler-Ross describes.

Alex Comfort suggests that a married couple prepare for bereavement — long before either one is faced with a threatening illness.

> Thinking through each other's possible deaths at least once—economically, practically, emotionally—isn't ghoulish or bad luck. It is loving, because each partner is considering the preservation of the other.... You normally take out insurance for a surviving partner. Take out survivor insurance by having a mutually agreed plan of reaction which will go into operation automatically if death should occur.... Oddly enough, you will not find it depressing in fact, although it sounds a downer in prospect. Women in particular, who, because of longer life and the fact they are often younger than their husbands, face a higher chance of being widows, are often deeply relieved once it has been done.*

Often, unspoken aspects of bereavement cause the most trouble, e.g., feelings of guilt or relief, or guilt about feeling relief, all pervaded by the desolation of loneliness. Ambivalent feelings and strong anger, even toward the one who has died, are common reactions, yet they are ones with which many people are uncomfortable. Time is needed to work through the experience: many weeks, perhaps many months. Sympathetic friends can help greatly, provided they neither dodge the real issues involved nor dwell upon them unhealthfully. Giving advice and trying to hurry a person through grief usually

*Taken from *A Good Age* by Alex Comfort . © Mitchell Beazley publishers LTD., 1976. Used by permission of Crown Publishers, Inc.

makes the grieving process more difficult and confusing. Various widow-to-widow (and widower) type programs have been initiated, some of them in churches. These programs help many people, but the decision to participate should be made by the grieving individual.

A problem of some widows has been called "husband sanctification" ("wife sanctification" would operate the same way). The departed husband continues to serve as part of her support system. She consults with him and tries to do as she feels he advises. It is essential that this person learn to rely on herself or himself or friends. As time wears on she or he must also learn to deal with reality, to rebuild life on a sound basis.

Another problem may be the reaction of adult children, as well as some relatives or friends, to new relationships formed by the surviving spouse, particularly those that may lead to courtship and marriage. These people may be motivated by their own grieving over the loss of a loved one and their resentment at what may appear to be insufficient respect. Sometimes their attitude reflects the belief, not necessarily valid in every case, that a person should be in mourning for at least a year. Sometimes, too, children and relatives may be concerned about financial issues, such as what will happen to their inheritance if the parent remarries. A new will, of course, can be drawn to meet such worries. It is important to talk frankly about all these problems, both with the family members and with the prospective new spouse.

Many widows, widowers, and others who have been bereaved need other kinds of assistance, as varying as their personalities and situations: financial help to assist with the rent, the mortgage, or food, at least during the initial period of shock; help with transportation, legal advice, or care of the house or car; social assistance, the opportunity for companionship with individuals and groups, so long as this is not imposed upon them. The deepest need is emotional, the listening ear of someone who understands and is ready to stand alongside one who has suffered loss. Will the church, as the fellowship of the resurrection, as a caring community, enter more fully into its ministry to the bereaved?

Loneliness brings pain to many older persons for reasons other than immediate bereavement, e.g. divorce, mental or physical illness, geographical isolation, rejection by other people, lack of close friends. Loneliness can cause illness and death. "Loneliness is not only pushing our culture to the breaking point, it is pushing our physical health to the breaking point," writes James J. Lynch, a specialist in psychosomatic medicine at the University of Maryland Medical School.

Reaffirming the importance of the family and restoring the caring relationship among friends and neighbors, not group therapies or encounter/sensitivity training, is where the solution of the problem lies, argues Dr. Lynch. Again, the challenge to the Christian congregation is obvious. For some lonely persons the congregation will have to be both family and community.

Death

Even though death is a natural and inescapable part of life, most people do very little thinking about it. A universal, often subconscious, fear of death has led persons and cultures, including our own, into different ways of denying it. Approximately half of all deaths in our country occur in large general hospitals and in nursing homes. In such surroundings it is typical that medical professionals are so preoccupied with keeping people alive that they allow the dying to go through their experience alone and isolated. These men and women, especially those who are older, may have been engaged already in a lonely struggle against slow chronic illness, or perhaps have endured extraordinary medical measures which have erected barriers between them and other persons.

Denial of death is encouraged in our culture by many of our funeral practices. The protection of the family from contact with the dead until embalming is completed, the soft music, the carpeted "funeral parlor," the use of euphemisms like "passed away" instead of "died" — these and other practices may make it difficult for the bereaved to face reality and work through the process of grief. It should be acknowledged, however, that many of the practices in funeral homes are helpful rather than offensive, especially when they provide full opportunity for pastors, family and friends to comfort and support one another.

Under the impact of the work of Dr. Elisabeth Kübler-Ross and others, people in our society are learning to talk about death. Indeed, the increasing popularity of this topic in some circles has made it something of a fad. It is to be hoped that concentration upon the subject of death will be matched by a comparable emphasis upon the later years of life which precede death. Dr. Robert N. Butler, Director of the National Institute on Aging (U.S.), says: "In truth, it is easier to manage the problem of death than the problem of living as an old person. Death is a dramatic, one-time crisis, while old age is a day-by-day and year-by-year confrontation with powerful external and internal forces, a bittersweet coming to terms with one's own personality and one's life."*

The readiness of people today to ask more open questions about death should lead both to a more honest facing of the basic issues of life and also to more mature and sensitive approaches to the dying patient. For example, there are increasing efforts to move the dying out of hospitals and into more normal surroundings, such as the hospices where professionals provide special treatment in an atmosphere of warmth, acceptance, and hope, and where children and grandchildren of patients are encouraged to spend time. These hospices are also showing ways in which it is practical to keep many dying persons at home. This can become more widespread when home care is supported by the financial arrangements of health care systems.

Programs are beginning to appear which train medical personnel and other professional people to deal with the ethical issues posed by death and the availability of sophisticated techniques for prolonging life, as well as to respond understandingly to the needs of the aging.

It is said that younger people fear death itself but older people fear the process of dying — the losses that attend it, the dangers of extended illness, pain or incapacity, the anxiety about becoming a burden to family or society, and the unresolved guilt feelings arising from their life

*Robert N. Butler, *Why Survive? Being Old in America* (New York: Harper & Row, 1975), p. 11. Reprinted by permission.

experiences. These new approaches offer promise of helping older adults as they face death — their own and that of their friends and loved ones.

Older men and women can be helped tremendously by family members and friends who are willing to listen sympathetically. Dr. Butler speaks of the importance of the life review. What many a listener thinks of as dull reminiscence is instead the universal process by which the older person strives to reinterpret what has happened in the past in terms of his or her present values. The guilt feelings, the unresolved conflicts, come out into the open, as they must. When a person dwells upon negative aspects of the past, the listener may be able to call attention to some of the positives. The man or woman engaged in the life review may experience a variety of emotional states, during some of which listening may be difficult. Nevertheless, the hoped-for outcome is integration of the person, an acceptance of one's life, the assurance of the forgiveness of sins. This basic experience can contribute greatly to the meaning and satisfaction of the later years as well as help the man or woman deal constructively with any trials that may be met on the way to death.

The new readiness in society to face death openly and to talk frankly about the issues it raises offers a fresh challenge to the church. The Christian faith makes no promise of a bland continuation of our life into an indefinite future. It sees death as "the wages of sin" and "the last enemy that shall be destroyed" (1 Corinthians 15:26). Jesus wept real tears at the tomb of Lazarus his friend. As he confronted his own death he was in agony — "his sweat was like drops of blood falling to the ground"

(Luke 22:44). The Christian faith takes death seriously, and then proclaims the good news that the sting of death is overcome by the resurrection of Christ, and that forgiveness and new life are granted to those who believe in the Risen One.

Seldom has the challenge been greater for the church to bring the resurrection faith to people. It should witness with clarity, power and fervor to the gospel that Christ has risen...and so shall we!

3 Living the Older Years in Health

Living The Older Years in Health

Older people require knowledge about their bodies as they develop and change through life. Seneca, the Roman philosopher, said that man does not die, but kills himself. This is another way of emphasizing the fact that individuals, by learning and taking personal responsibility, can enhance both the quality and the length of their lives. Each person, by becoming "health educated," will learn to adopt and practice the preventive health measures that are necessary for health maintenance.

Health is defined by the World Health Organization as "not merely the absence of disease and infirmity but a state of complete physical, mental and social well-being." Health is not an isolated matter; it is related to all aspects of human life.

A Health Philosophy

What priority do individuals give to their own health — at any age? At an older age? Is good health merely taken for granted until one begins to lose it? In a recent CBS-TV Special, it was reported that retired people rank health above finances as an important concern. Elmer Otte, a writer on pre-retirement planning, says that the single most important thing you must save for your retirement security is your health. In the summary of research findings from a longitudinal study made by Duke University health maintenance was placed first among three factors in longevity.

How important is health to people in their middle years and in youth? We know that good health in later years depends very much on what happens earlier. This is stressed by Dr. Robert N. Butler, of the National Institute on Aging, when he says that sound health practices cannot begin in adult life, but should begin with prenatal and infant care. This underscores also the importance of the care of health in youth and the middle years. It points up the necessity for increased emphasis on prevention, particularly health education. Some ways to improve health: positive public action, change of behavior, and a health care system based on pre-payment rather than fee-for-service.

Some Facts About the Health of Older Adults

A large majority of individuals 65 and over have better health than many believe. More than 80 percent move about independently, and only about 4 percent reside in institutions such as nursing homes and hospitals.

Older persons, however, are more vulnerable than others to the onslaught of diseases, especially those that are chronic. The most prevalent include: arthritis (27 percent of persons 65 years of age and older), heart disease (15 percent), and high blood pressure (13 percent). The elderly are also subject to cancer and to mental conditions. It should be pointed out that, although modern medical science has had much to do with lengthening the life span, it has achieved this chiefly by conquering the infectious diseases which commonly attack children. Many more people now survive childhood and live to old age, where they find that chronic illness remains a major problem.

Although many older adults have one or more chronic health problems, most of them learn how to function with or in spite of these conditions.

The previous chapter stressed the importance of distinguishing between disease and the natural changes that belong to the aging process. Much of what we think of as aging today is actually disease and not a part of natural aging. Even in the case of chronic diseases it is essential to separate fact from fiction. There are members of the medical profession who often write off older persons as "senile" (a very loosely-used word) when they are actually suffering from conditions that can be reversed or modified. It is wrong to withhold the gifts of skilled medical care with the question, "What do you expect at your age?"

Problem or Challenge

When we look at health from a financial standpoint, we find that persons 65 and over use one-fourth of the health dollar, occupy one-third of the hospital beds and almost all the long-term beds, consume most of the home-care services, and spend two to three times as much on health care as does any other age group, according to Leslie S. Libow. However, a large number of them are poor and thus have less money for health and medical care. This is true especially of older women. A recent program on the NBC-TV Today Show gives the information that six out of ten women over 65 are in poverty. With more people now living longer, and the average life span lengthening, the problem is growing. Today's girl babies can expect to live to age 81 and boy babies to 72.

These projections highlight the size and importance of future health care needs among older adults. Such needs increase progressively in older years. Costs, for which older people and their families will have to pay at least a part, will continue to rise. In Canada, medical and hospital expenses of those 65 and over are covered without hardship under the Hospital Insurance and Diagnostic Act and the Medical Care Act.

Attitudes and Health

The Influence of Societal Attitudes

Noting that the prophet Daniel at the age of 80 was thrown into the lion's den by his enemies, Katie E. Weib suggests that today many older people get pushed into the lion's den of old age by a society that doesn't know what to do with them. It retires some before they are ready, shoves some into nursing homes because no one wants to take care of them, and forces others to live on inadequate pensions. The lions of rejection, loneliness and boredom lurk nearby. Such societal attitudes, among other effects, are bound to reduce the potential of older men and women to enjoy robust physical and mental health.

Here we see once more the negative image of aging which pervades many parts of our society. Some even may say that money spent on the aged is money thrown away since these old people will likely not live much longer. It is hoped that this attitude is not widespread, for each man and woman is a human being, a person to be treated with dignity. Our youth-oriented times tend to demean the qualities of age and to tempt older people to try to look and act younger than they are. Consider the phenomenon called "ageism"— an automatic prejudice toward the elderly solely on the basis of chronological age—and the paternalistic efforts to do things for older people rather than open up full opportunities for them to participate freely in church and community.

To what extent can the elderly themselves work to change destructive attitudes like these? Have they not shared in the creation of the negative image? Do they not often accept it too readily? But surely older adults can have a profound constructive influence. Not long ago a group of them spent a week at a Lutheran retreat center. They were served in the dining hall by some young people who had been counselors for youth during earlier weeks. At the end of the week one of the young men was heard to say: "If we can come to old age with as much enthusiasm as this group, we will not fear it."

There are many stories of significant achievements by older men and women. It should be recognized that the well-known achievers are not as unusual as many suppose. Large numbers of less known persons are active and busy in constructive pursuits and many of those who are more passive are entirely capable of becoming more fully engaged in remunerative employment, volunteer service, or meaningful leisure pursuits. The example set by vital, alert older adults can go far toward nourishing a more positive image of themselves and of the aging process.

When congregations and communities develop new concepts of the dignity and worth of people of all ages, including the elderly, long steps will have been taken in the direction of greater justice and fulfillment for all — and better physical and mental health.

The Influence of Personal Attitudes

Good mental health means the capacity to thrive rather than merely survive, the capacity for creativity, curiosity and surprise as well as fulfillment in life. How one feels about one's self and one's attitude toward being old are important to health.

Ethel Shanas, of the University of Illinois, stresses the significance of attitudes for health in her report on studies of old people in Denmark, Britain, and the United States.

> Old age is accompanied by a decline in physical fitness and an increasing experience with body aches and pains. Each person makes his own accommodation to his changing body. Some people become preoccupied with their bodily state, and each ache and pain is magnified. It is these persons who become health pessimists and report their health as poor when objective indices suggest their health is fairly good. Other people seem to ignore physical discomfort. It is these persons who are the health optimists, who insist they are well in the face of appalling physical distress or who overemphasize their physical fitness and the extent to which their health is better than the health of other people.*

The way in which people bear their ills depends much more on their state of mind than on the gravity of the ills. Sometimes professional help is necessary when older persons suffer from hypochondriasis.

*Ethel Shanas: "The Psychology of Health," in Ethel Shanas, et al., *Old People in Three Industrial Societies* (New York: Atherton Press, 1968), p. 36.

How individuals feel about themselves may influence their involvement in alcohol and other drug problems and in suicide.

Alcohol and Other Drug Abuse

Alcoholism, in addition to causing social and financial problems, is a major killer through liver disease, highway accidents and crime. It frequently develops in connection with grief, loneliness and feelings of uselessness and worthlessness.

Karl Schneider, in his study program, *Alcoholism and Addiction*, emphasizes the prevalence of alcohol abuse among older persons. He mentions, for instance, that:

> Thirty percent of all calls made to the Drug Hotline in Browne County, New York, were by older persons. One community survey revealed that 30 percent of the calls to alcohol information and referral centers came from persons over 55. Services in the community were not adequate to meet the needs of older problem drinkers. As a conservative estimate, the number of older problem drinkers in the U. S. is clearly in excess of one million persons.*

Schneider discusses this subject more fully in his study book, and also calls attention to the dangers frequently encountered by older people as a result of taking alcohol in combination with other drugs.

Alex Comfort states that alcohol:

- is fatally incompatible with many medications;
- is often a covert form of suicide;
- impairs brain performance;
- increases risk of falling — a major danger to the old;

* Karl A. Schneider, *Alcoholism and Addiction* (Philadelphia: Fortress Press, 1976), p. 10. Reprinted by permission.

- is a dangerous drug for people who are lonely, sick or have life problems — far more dangerous than heroin because it is around and well-meaning friends are pushers; and
- is costly.*

In their effort to get relief from pain or tension older people often buy over-the-counter drugs in addition to their prescription medicines. Some take drugs prescribed for a friend or family member, or take old and new prescriptions together. Some find it difficult to keep track of their assigned doses, with the result that they take too much or too little, or mix medicines. Older adults, like other people, sometimes take drugs in order to feel better or get through the day. We hear that old persons in nursing homes are frequently given drugs to keep them quiet and passive. And, unfortunately, there are physicians who find it simpler to give pills than to listen to complaints and work out treatment plans that may include nutritious diet, physical exercise, or social activities. We need to be aware of and on guard against these abuses.

A Positive Approach to Health

Elmer Otte suggests: "Have love—give love. Have something to get up for every day. Remain important to somebody. Accept the compassion of others for your own well-being and repay such concern with warm empathy toward them."

Often upon retirement friends congratulate the retiree and say, "Now you can take it easy, you have earned a rest." But the medical advice is just the opposite: stay active, stay busy; good health and successful aging are fostered by purposeful activity. Unfortunately, many older persons seem to want to avoid activity, saying that

*Taken from *A Good Age* by Alex Comfort. © Mitchell Beazley publishers LTD., 1976. Used by permission of Crown Publishers, Inc.

they have done their part. Some even want to be entertained by others. But active older people should help their contemporaries find constructive things to do. Many of them have skills to share, and are glad when they have the good health and ability that enables them to minister to others.

Caring for the Body

Physical Activity

"Exercise," says Joseph Hrachovec, "is the closest thing to an anti-aging pill now available. It is free for the doing." Yet, according to surveys, far less than half the people 60 and over engage in any systematic exercise. Edward Stanley, Earl of Derby, said in December 1873 that those who think they do not have time for bodily exercise will sooner or later have to find time for illness.

Walking is considered a very good exercise for older adults in that the use of the legs in exercise expedites the return flow of blood to the heart. Exercises advised as good for older adults are: swimming, dancing, bicycling, running. Doing chores around the house and gardening are also good, but there is need for daily systematic activities. However, older persons are advised to get medical advice about the type of exercise in which to engage, particularly after a period of inactivity.

The President's Council on Physical Fitness and Sports is taking action to improve the situation of very low physical fitness practices among older adults. The Council devoted the April 1977 issue of its *Physical Fitness Research Digest* to exercise and aging. This publication contains references to various researchers showing the importance of exercise and the ability of older people to learn exercises. The Administration on Aging has published an exercise program for older Americans, *The Fitness Challenge...in the Later Years.* This program lays out a system of exercises.

There is evidence that physically active persons are less likely to experience heart attacks. In fact, Dr. Butler says that exercise reduces the risk of heart attacks and enhances survival after an attack. Through exercise the heart, which is a muscle, is strengthened and enabled to do its work more efficiently. Exercise can also help a person to cope with life's stresses. Some say the greatest benefit of physical activity may be the degree of independence it gives.

The upsurge in physical activity among adults in the late 1960's, one writer observes, coincided with the beginning of the decline in heart attacks. This is noteworthy, he goes on to say, even though other things such as blood pressure control and more attention to low-fat foods in diets may also be contributing to the decline. Even though there has been a downturn in deaths from heart attacks, the number is still frightening. Exercise should be taken *regularly* and in accordance with the needs of the individual.

Dental Care

Good dental care is also as essential for older adults as for those at younger ages. This includes regular dental check-ups for inspection and cleaning, suitable diet, regular daily cleaning of one's own teeth. Those who need dentures should persist until they fit, for having dentures that do not fit makes chewing more difficult and eating less enjoyable. Frequent adjustments may be needed, since the mouth may change rather rapidly in later years. But alterations should be made by the dentist; individuals should not "whittle" on their dentures. Dentures need daily cleaning and care just as natural teeth do. Good dental care, including well-fitting dentures, is conducive to good feeling and appearance.

Nutrition

Another area crucial for all ages, but particularly for older adults, is nutrition. Dr. Butler says that Americans have an intake of too many calories, too much sugar and far too much salt. Perhaps more than any other life-style element, good nutrition is critical for well-being in the later years of life.

It is known that many older people have poor eating habits. Some reasons for this are: loneliness (they do not like to eat alone or cook for one person), poverty (for a good many), less taste appeal for food (some suffer some atrophy of taste buds in later years), lack of hunger (they don't take much exercise), and poor education about nutrition and foods, especially about particular foods which do not agree with them and about foods they need, such as those that prevent constipation.

Various organizations, including some congregations, now organize social programs for older adults. Many of these include a meal, served monthly, weekly, or more often. Congregate meals, supported by the federal government, are served at least five days a week in many communities. Older adults assist in planning, preparing and serving these meals. Information about nutrition, meal-planning and other food questions is sometimes a part of these programs. Meals-on-wheels, meals taken to homes of shut-ins or those unable to prepare, is a service in a number of communities, mainly urban. Many members of congregations serve as volunteers in the meals-on-wheels service as well as in other programs. Frequently, these volunteers are older adults.

As the years go by a person requires fewer calories. Therefore, in order to remain at the same weight, one should eat less. One source says that a person at age 65 needs 20 percent fewer calories than at age 25. In case a physician has prescribed a special diet, the individual may need further explanation of the prescription and assistance in planning the specific food items. Such help is available from hospital dietitians, public health nurses, or other qualified personnel.

Currently there is an upsurge of eating out, and we are told that this family practice is likely to increase. Too often the choice of restaurant is the type that serves fast-food meals. Some of these fast-foods have only limited nutritional value; or, as often happens, the consumer ends up with an unbalanced diet. The taste acquired for the fast-foods may continue into adult life and later years, thus eventually adding to the problem of poor nutrition of older persons.

Community Resources and Services

In order for individuals to have choices in health and medical services, these services have to be available and accessible, and at prices the consumer can pay. Some communities have limited numbers of professional personnel, particularly those with qualifications for serving the older adults. In Canada, for example, there are few doctors skilled in treating and caring for older people. Canada has 1,000 pediatricians and only 25 geriatricians.

In the United States, the American Medical Association lists 13,000 office-based pediatricians but keeps no separate tabulation of geriatricians. Contact with medical schools in 1962 showed little interest in establishing courses in geriatric medicine. But in 1970, when 99 schools were contacted, 49 made some mention of the subject, according to Robert Butler. Now with the establishment of the National Institute on Aging, it is expected that the situation will improve rapidly.

Although medical and health services may exist in a community, some older persons need transportation to get to them. In some areas this is being provided by volunteers, often other older adults. In others an effort is made to place the sites of services nearer the residences of older adults. For example, clinics are being held in retirement centers for the use of persons in the neighborhoods as well as residents of the centers.

Services are often organized on a one-time basis in connection with community functions such as a health fair. Tests for diabetes, blood pressure and other services are given. A women's organization in one congregation used the skills of one of its members, a retired nurse, who checked blood pressure at meetings.

Until recently emphasis had been put on institutional care and services by physicians. Home health programs are a way to enable individuals to continue living in their own homes if they so choose. These services, ordered by a physician, may include nursing care, physical therapy, nurse aide services and sometimes others. There is a new stress on the contributions to health that can be made by other categories of professionals, paraprofessionals, and even family members.

Self-care is another development that seems to be gaining attention. Many persons have already practiced self-help in connection with the treatment of their diabetic conditions, after instruction by professionals. These new trends are due to such factors as increased costs, the realization that hospitals should be reserved for the critically ill and those who need special treatment, an increased population demanding more health care, and the fact that many can be served adequately at home and by other types of personnel rendering a variety of services.

Although medical and health services are inadequate in most communities, more are available than are being used. Screening programs are useful in discovering such conditions as diabetes, glaucoma, cancer and stroke, so that they can be treated as early as possible. In many communities health departments or voluntary agencies provide these services at little or no cost. But they are not fully used, especially by older adults. Some communities are making special efforts to get the elderly to take advantage of them. Congregate meals programs and meetings of organizations, including church organizations, offer particularly good opportunities for making these medical and health services known.

Older persons sometimes become incapacitated suddenly. Many of them have made no arrangements for the handling of their affairs in such a crisis, a type of crisis that is familiar to many parish pastors, retirement home managers, and friends in the neighborhood. It is highly recommended, therefore, that every older man or woman designate a family member or friend to take necessary actions. This may involve "power of attorney" or some other arrangement. It is particularly important for elderly persons who have no family members nearby.

It is encouraging that the church and society in general seem to be more aware of the special needs of handicapped persons, many of whom are elderly. More frequently today we hear of efforts to adjust programs and modify facilities to enable the handicapped to function independently.

Supportive Services and the Church's Role

Not all health care needs can be met by medical and professional health services. Many older adults need supportive services, such as assistance with housekeeping, grocery shopping, minor repairs around the house, and transportation. Such programs can enable older persons to choose to remain at home when ill, or to come home from a hospital earlier than they could otherwise. Despite the fact that the need for supportive services appears obvious, their relatively slow development underscores the urgency of intensive efforts to initiate them and convince society of their value.

A critical and most important role is played by the church. It has a larger number of older adults in its constituency than does any other organization. According to studies at Duke University, older people believe that church and religion are vital. A congregation can contribute to constructive, healthful living in many ways. It can involve its older adults in meaningful activities related to the church's ministry with its members and community. It can anticipate the retirement of its members and guide them into a needed service satisfying to them. The congregation may wish to provide a coordinator of volunteers (paid or volunteer) to assist in this work. It may also provide opportunities for its members to learn about their changing health needs and about the various health resources and services available, as well as the procedures for their use. For example, in one community, (Guilford County, North Carolina), the Public Health Department issued a folder listing the various general, geriatric and special (cancer, etc.) clinic services helpful for older adults. The folder also included the following list of "What Every Older Person Needs":

*someone to care for and love him/her,

*a purpose that gives direction and significance to her/his life,

*a place to live in wholesome surroundings with fresh air, sun and quiet,

*community responsibilities and activities that bring out his/her best,

*an opportunity to learn new things and keep flexible in mind and spirit,

*a diet that meets her/his individual requirements,

*a combination of exercise and rest that suits his/her condition,

*medical care to maintain health and well-being at her/his highest possible level,

*a sufficient variety in life to add interest and keep him/her mentally alert, and

*a triumphant religious faith or philosophy to give serenity and peace of mind.

4 Living Arrangements

Living Arrangements

Adequate living arrangements for older adults include far more than a building with four walls and a roof. Good housing and good location are among the essential ingredients to satisfy deep human needs for *independence, security, identity,* and *well-being.* Actually, a full concept of living arrangements involves even more: "aesthetics, economics, community planning, city administration, the structuring of a neighborhood, and the character of a community."

Mr. Abraham Isserman, co-chairman of the Section on Housing at the 1971 White House Conference on Aging, discussed how these four human needs influence what people do about living arrangements. The need for "independence" cannot be met unless the elderly have housing at a cost that enables them to maintain a decent living standard in all respects. The need for "security" cannot be satisfied if a person cannot go out on the street for fear of being mugged or run down by heavy traffic, or cannot get to the bathroom safely in the middle of the night. The sense of "identity" cannot be fostered unless the older man or woman can exercise some choice of environment and enjoy familiar furniture, cherished possessions, and pets. To facilitate the "well-being" of the elderly, housing must be within easy reach, insofar as possible, of family, friends, church, entertainment, stores, a library, medical, personal and social services. It must encourage, not discourage, continuing personal contacts and involvement of older adults in life around them.

The basic concept is that of "home." Home is probably the single most important element in the life of an older person. He or she probably spends more time there than does anyone else over the age of five. Home is being able to give and receive invitations, having privacy with chosen friends, and being alone when this is desired. Unfortunately, a large number of older people live under arrangements which hardly suggest "home" to outside observers — single rooms in rundown hotels, worn-out shacks in remote rural areas, institutions of various kinds. Although these places are indeed "home" to many of these people, their situation only underscores the responsibility of society, including churches, to enable the elderly to have living arrangements which meet fundamental needs for independence, security, identity and well-being.

When we take seriously the significance of home, it is not hard to understand why the elderly often resist moving, even from what appears to others to be undesirable quarters. A move would put them in unfamiliar surroundings and likely among total strangers. If the move is to an institution, both the prospect and the actual move may be a crushing experience unless special efforts are made to prepare the way.

A Variety of Living Arrangements

Living arrangements should be as appropriate as possible to a person's individual needs and circumstances at any given time. Since responsibility for this rests basically with the man and/or woman involved, a maximum of opportunity for her or his responsible decision-making should be encouraged. But there are thousands of situations where it is necessary, not only for families, but for communities (including churches) and public agencies to assist.

Independent Living

Most older people live with their spouses in their own homes. A large number of individuals continue to live in their own homes after being widowed.

For those who have sufficient funds this is the most comfortable arrangement. Probably they already have good housing, and are able to maintain the house and grounds and employ people to do chores. Furthermore, in case declining health limits their activity, they can secure the medical and home care services needed to retain considerable independence. They are even able to move elsewhere if the neighborhood changes or they want to be nearer their families or in a warmer climate.

For those who do not have sufficient funds, however, the story is different. Many persons have had inadequate incomes throughout their careers; others have become poor for the first time upon retirement. Homeowners in both groups frequently have substandard housing, especially in rural areas. They cannot afford major repairs and improvements, and, if they reach the point where they cannot care for their property, they have great difficulty employing others to do it for them. Likewise, they lack the resources to purchase the services of nurses, homemakers or others who might enable them to live in their homes with reasonable self-sufficiency even with some physical handicaps. Although they own their own homes, perhaps with no mortgages, property taxes require an inordinate percentage of their funds. Sometimes the changes that take place in neighborhoods leave these older adults isolated from families and friends, familiar stores, doctors and other services. Yet, they usually find it difficult to consider moving to other communities.

Indeed, the supply of housing designed for older adults is severely limited. Single family homes within their income levels are hard to find and buy, and condominiums are beyond the financial range of all but a relatively affluent minority. Some turn to mobile homes, which are becoming more popular especially in the South and Southwest.

Planned retirement communities, which have arisen during recent decades, have often been controversial. Many people have been critical of them, usually because they feel that such communities segregate the elderly in synthetic surroundings, "retirement ghettos." Others ask whether this practice is really different from the tendency of young couples with children to concentrate in single-age suburban developments. A number of studies of residents of retirement communities have had quite positive results. Many of the older people living in them appreciate the security provided and the companionship with men and women who have had similar experiences. At any rate those who wish to live in these communities, and can afford it, should have the freedom to make this choice.

A large number of older persons rent their housing, but most of them experience great difficulty keeping up with steadily rising rents when they are on fixed incomes. In recent years, in the face of abuse by some landlords, many low-income and middle-income tenants (of all ages) and elderly renters on fixed incomes have begun to counteract the power of landlords by means of such techniques as rent strikes and court challenges. One prominent organization helping them to channel their strength is the National Tenants Organization. The trend is toward increased participation of older persons in this kind of activity.

Public housing in the United States has been created primarily by the federal government but also by state and municipal governments. Even the federal programs are administered by local housing authorities in accordance with the Housing Act of 1937. Because these local authorities do not have sufficient funds, they have often been forced to evict tenants who have gotten behind in their rent payments, a practice which has been particularly hard on the elderly. Even so-called low income public housing costs too much for a large number of poor older adults, who must settle for inferior quarters. There are many other older people, of course, whose income is too high to enable them to live in public housing, which sets upper limits. Aside from these problems, public housing is not being built fast enough to accommodate all who could use it. And much of it that does exist is poorly maintained and poorly protected, with the result that residents live in unattractive, unsanitary, and often dangerous conditions.

Semi-Independent Living

What happens when disabilities limit activity and make it difficult to care for oneself and the house? Unless the situation is of such a nature as to justify it, institutionalization must not be regarded as the only answer. There are other approaches.

Many older adults continue living in *their own homes or at least their own communities* with the help of supportive services, such as meals-on-wheels, visiting nurses, homemaker-home health services, chore assistance, telephone reassurance, and visiting (for fuller discussion of supportive services see Chapter VI). In some cases a social caseworker based in a social agency or institution working with the elderly makes regular contact and arranges services that are appropriate for particular individuals. Such a program can be sponsored by communities, public agencies like the Area Agencies on Aging (U.S.A.), voluntary organizations, or churches/synagogues. This approach can and should be developed and extended.

Other older adults are able to live semi-independently in *the homes of members of their families*. Although tensions are always possible in these situations, such arrangements have proved acceptable in many instances, especially when earlier relationships between generations have been constructive. Greater freedom and better relationships in the family are encouraged by provision of a separate room or apartment, possibly with cooking facilities, for the older person or persons.

It may not prove to be mutually beneficial, Minna Field emphasizes, if adult children invite ailing parents into their homes primarily because of guilt feelings or fear of what other people will think. The decision must be on firmer ground, with careful consideration given to the personalities involved, the size of the house, the needs of the children and young people, the health and financial circumstances of the host family, and the degree to which the move might cut off the older parent from significant friends and familiar associations and reduce his or her independence and dignity. Many adult children are not aware of the supportive services available in their own communities, which may make a crucial difference in the decisions to be made.

In some areas *foster homes* for older persons are available. A semi-independent man or woman lives in the home of a family or individual who contracts to care for the older adult. It is important that this kind of living arrangement be under the auspices of a competent agency, which will require that those in charge be given effective training and be monitored regularly.

Congregate Living Facilities

The various types of living arrangements for older adults should not be called "alternatives to institutionalization." All arrangements are seen in better perspective if we speak rather of "institutionalization as an alternative." For persons who will benefit from some form of congregate living facilities, numerous options are available. Some are under public auspices, supported from tax funds. Others are proprietary or commercial, operated as business enterprises.

Still others are not-for-profit facilities. Among the not-for-profit facilities those which are sponsored by churches have, generally, a reputation for high quality services. Nevertheless, the churches must be diligent in monitoring their work to ensure that they continue to meet the most exacting standards.

One type of congregate living facility is *group housing,* where several ambulatory older persons live together in a house, in which live-in management staff is responsible for maintenance, meals, and other necessary care. An example is provided by the "Share-a-Home" residences in Central Florida, which are now being established in other areas. The people who live there are free to come and go, see their own doctors, worship where they please, and have guests for dinner. They share monthly costs of food, staff, and utilities, and are in charge of running "their home." In this case, a non-profit, volunteer-staffed organization, Share-a-Homes of America, Inc. helps establish new residences and stands by to assist existing ones. For elderly men and women who can no longer live alone yet don't require constant medical care, it may mean the difference between life in a family-type setting and confinement to an institution.

Another type of congregate facility is the *residential care home*. Often initiated by churches, these are growing in number. They provide attractive, usually apartment-style housing. Although there is freedom for the individual or couple to live independently and to go and come at will, common facilities are on the premises for dining, medical care, fellowship, recreation and often worship. Various financial arrangements are practiced in different places.

The *intermediate care home,* which provides care under the supervision of a registered nurse, is designed for the frail elderly who do not need constant medical attention but require a place to live and the security of knowing that help is near. This kind of home — the oldest, most widespread and most familiar of congregate living accommodations — makes available to its residents common dining, recreation and worship as long as they are able to utilize such services. It should permit as much freedom of movement and personal privacy (both inside and beyond the facility) as its residents can safely exercise. Such a home differs from the skilled care home in that the decision to enter it involves more choice by the prospective resident. The choice, however, is only relatively free because there is no acceptable alternative. This may be so even if adult children have readily offered their own homes, because the elderly person prefers to be dependent upon strangers whose job it is to provide care rather than upon daughters or sons.

A fourth type of congregate facility is the *skilled care home.* This provides the most constant and intensive nursing care. Normally, the physician makes referral to the institution, and very often the patient is transferred there from a hospital. Health care facilities such as this will always be needed for the chronically ill. Although supportive services of various kinds will enable large numbers of older persons to continue living in their communities, often till death, these services cannot eliminate the normal dependencies of old age. In fact, the increase in the population of people in their upper 70's, 80's and 90's will require more and more skilled nursing beds.

We must be concerned, therefore, with the quality of this kind of care, which has been the subject of scandalous revelations and intense debate during the last few years. And, beyond the quality of physical care, we must be actively interested in the human climate of these institutions, whether they be under public, commercial, voluntary or church auspices.

An emotional problem not often dealt with is the traumatic experience of the older person whose husband or wife, sister or brother, or close friend has been admitted to a skilled-care home. Financially speaking, pension and health benefit programs do not allow enough money to sustain the person outside in addition to the cost of care of the institutionalized spouse. In terms of emotional need, all those who are close to one who has entered nursing care need sensitive support from the extended family, the church and the community. Some church institutions and agencies are beginning to develop programs to fill this need. They are helping families deal with feelings of guilt, anger and frustration, and the anxiety about what others are thinking regarding the decisions they make.

Responsible Decision Making

Choosing a Retirement Location and Housing

When Mr. Baxter retired from his position in New Jersey, he and his wife moved to the east coast of Florida. Before long they realized they had not taken time to consider all the factors involved in relocating. Unhappy in Florida, they returned to their New Jersey community, and bought a small house. There they lived for two years; but, since the property tax was too burdensome, they put their house up for sale and sold it before they had another place to go. They took a train to Sarasota, Florida, which they had never seen, and looked at houses and apartments. Five days later they were back, unsuccessful in their search for housing in Sarasota. They had to take a second-floor apartment temporarily in a neighboring New Jersey town until their new house in a retirement village in New Jersey was ready for them. They appear at last to be settled and content.

The story of the Baxters illustrates a wrong way to make decisions. They acted too quickly several times, without adequately weighing factors important to their future happiness. They were fortunate to have enough money to correct their mistakes. Many other people who have made hasty decisions have been forced to live with the consequences.

The selection of living arrangements calls for well-thought-out decisions on the part of the older adult or adults. Most people prefer to stay where they are as long as they can. But a relocation may become a necessity because of reduced income, decline in physical or mental health, loneliness caused by death of a mate, difficulty in enduring a rigorous climate, or changes in the neighborhood. Situations like these may force many men and women to move soon after retirement. In a large number of instances there are likely to be other relocations as conditions alter with the passing of the years.

Although family pressures often have influence, we usually assume that persons approaching retirement have a clear responsibility to decide whether to stay where they are or move, and, if they move, where they should go. Each man or woman or couple should draw up a list of criteria well in advance of decision time.

Things to Consider Before Moving

1. What are the advantages and disadvantages of remaining in the house and neighborhood where you have been living?
2. Is your house now suitable, or can it be prepared readily, for the requirements of retirement living? For example, are the grounds reasonably level, is the house readily accessible to the garage/driveway, would it be possible to arrange for living on one floor?
3. Is the tax rate one that can be met within your retirement income?
4. What are your feelings about the house and neighborhood?
5. Might you prefer to live elsewhere in your present community?
6. If you wish to move to another community, on what basis can you make a wise decision?

   *your own background, interests, talents,

   *nearness to children, other family members or old friends,

   *prospective neighbors and neighborhood,

   *climate and/or scenic appeal,

   *nearness to a church with which you would like to identify,

   *cultural events, a library, and/or recreational opportunities in keeping with your interest; will

you be able to engage in your favorite craft or hobby?

* cost of living in the area in relation to your anticipated income; is there any way (e.g. community master plan) by which you can estimate what the future tax rate will be?

* accessibility to doctors, hospitals, and special health facilities appropriate to your particular needs.

7. What type of housing appeals to you? What kind will you be able to afford? Detached housing — purchased or rented? Apartment — rented, condominium, public housing? Group (communal) living arrangement? Retirement community? Mobile home?

In choosing the location and housing for the years after retirement it would be wise for an older adult to spend some time in a prospective community during more than one season if possible. This would help avoid the danger of seeing only the good points concerning that area. Furthermore, it may be helpful to talk about plans and ideas with a third person whose judgment is respected.

Every person is unique. No one plan, regardless of how good it is, fits every situation. Individuals must consider their own needs and desires, and those of anyone else who expects to share their living arrangements. Couples, for example, sometimes have conflicts over what they want. After fair evaluation of all factors, they must make the best-informed, most responsible decision of which they are capable. After they have made it, since it will not be ideal in every respect, they should accept it and build their new life where they are.

If and when the time comes for older persons to make a move because of ill health or handicap, they may be vulnerable to the efforts of well-meaning friends, relatives, or adult children to make their decisions for them. Yet, unless disabilities actually limit their capacities, they are likely to be quite capable of making up their minds, perhaps with sympathetic and objective help from someone in sorting out the issues. In many cases, a skilled social caseworker, pastor, or other trained counselor will best be able to assist the elderly to make a sound decision. Older adults should be expected to exercise maximum freedom of choice all along the way, to determine what will be best for themselves and their families.

Choosing a Nursing Home

Admission to a skilled nursing care home often results from the recommendations of the hospital and doctors as part of the total treatment of the patient's illness, and the older person may not have much to say in the matter. Nevertheless, the deep need for the recognition of dignity and for as much independence as can be preserved requires that the older man or woman be part of the decision to the greatest extent possible. Here, too, a competent caseworker can help, and can also facilitate necessary decision-making by the family.

The church can render an important service by having individual or group sessions which help older persons and their families look ahead to admission to congregate living facilities. Pastors and social ministry leaders should keep an up-to-date file on the resources that exist in the church and the community to respond to the needs of older adults who must think in terms of such special living arrangements. If application is to be made to a government facility or a proprietary nursing home, it will be helpful for a pastor or another person to accompany the older man or woman through the process. Sometimes it may be necessary to put pressure on an agency to find ways of "cutting red tape."

How should an older person or family proceed in choosing a nursing home? Shop around in advance of immediate need. And be sure to consider alternatives to a nursing home. It may be that circumstances dictate that the older man or woman can remain at home with the assistance of homemakers, visiting nurses, or relatives who can care for the house, prepare meals, shop, and provide essential transportation.

But suppose a skilled nursing care home appears to be the best answer. On what basis does one make a selection? Here are some questions that might be asked (they should be tailored according to the situation of the individual involved):

Things to Consider When Choosing a Nursing Home

1. Does it provide the kind of care that suits the need, or the need that may appear later?
2. Is the home licensed by the state? This is a legal requirement but not necessarily an indication of reliability.
3. Is it certified for Medicare and Medicaid? If it is not,

the home is not receiving any federal funds.

4. What is the actual cost? Does the monthly rate cover everything, or are there unanticipated "extras"?
5. When was the last inspection made? When was the last federal inspection made? How often is the facility inspected?
6. Does the home require a complete physical examination before entrance or immediately thereafter? Is there also a questionnaire to be filled out dealing with such matters as the resident's interests, hobbies and favorite pastimes?
7. If the resident's personal physician will not continue care after entrance, does the home require a written transferral from that doctor to one serving the home?
8. Does the home have emergency admission arrangements with one or more of the general hospitals in the area?
9. Does the home have regular dental services? Are they "extras"?
10. Who owns the home? Is it a church or fraternal organization? (Sometimes a profit making home has a religious sounding name but is not recognized by a religious body.) Is it a physician or pharmacist, or someone who may have a conflict of interest or whose decisions may be unduly influenced by the profit motive?
11. Does the home require an entrance contract? If so, does the contract provide for a return of property if the patient leaves the home? Always have the entrance contract checked by a lawyer.
12. What are the qualifications of the administrator, who

is the key to the operation of the home?

13. Is a registered nurse on duty full-time on every shift? What are the qualifications and attitudes of the nurses and other workers?
14. How large is the nursing staff in proportion to the number of residents?
15. Are licensed practical nurses graduates of approved schools of practical nursing?
16. How large is the entire staff — nurses, doctors, kitchen personnel, laundry workers, maintenance men, etc? The national average is one staff member to every three beds.
17. How many patients are bedridden? If the number seems too large, the reason may be inadequate staff.
18. Is there an in-service training program for nurses' aides, thus indicating the home's desire to improve the quality of care?
19. Is there good rapport between the staff and the residents?
20. Does the home have a regular, qualified dietitian? Is the kitchen clean and well-equipped? Ask to see the kitchen.
21. Is the menu posted and followed? Are there different diets for residents who require them? Does the staff eat the same food as the residents?
22. Are the residents clean? Is their hair neat, clean and combed? Are their fingernails and toenails clean and cut? Is there an extra charge for washing hair or cutting nails?
23. Are the bedrooms neat and clean? Is there a urine odor

in the home — or a heavy cover-up odor?

24. Are the emergency buzzers within easy reach of the residents? Do staff members respond promptly and politely?
25. Do staff members show a positive attitude toward residents? Do they treat them respectfully as adults or do they refer to them as if they were children? Are the husbands and wives permitted to room together and/or be together in privacy, if they wish?
26. Do residents have regular channels through which to express grievances or influence the policies and practices of the home? Is there a residents' council, and/or access by residents to the board of directors?
27. Does the home have a disaster plan with assigned exit routes clearly posted? Are there periodic rehearsals?
28. What provision is made for worship in the nursing home? Chaplaincy service? Transportation to churches in the community?
29. Are residents who are physically able encouraged and assisted to participate in events and activities outside the home? Are they provided transportation to polling places or given absentee ballots if unable to travel?
30. Are families and friends of residents made welcome, and assisted to visit with reasonable freedom and to confer with staff members as needed? Does the home have a policy of notifying relatives when there is a change in a resident's condition? How soon?

This list of questions, based upon a list in a booklet prepared by Citizens for Better Care, of Detroit, Michigan, and supplemented by Tamerra Moeller, could be extended indefinitely. It emphasizes, however, the importance of investigating and planning ahead, if confronted by such an important decision as the choice of a nursing home.

From time to time we encounter the difficult situation in which an elderly infirm person refuses to make or accept a decision which appears to be in her or his own best interest. In such instances, the family members or friends, the pastor or other counselor must be certain not simply to project her or his own feelings into the life of an older adult. What if huge piles of old newspapers and magazines, along with three or four pet cats, are repulsive to the would-be intervener? This may be the life-style with which the older persons feels at home. The counselor must be exceedingly slow to force a change lest he or she violate that person's freedom of choice.

If, however, the elderly man or woman is so debilitated as to do things that endanger life or health, his or her own, or those of other people, other measures become necessary. A competent agency of social service or law enforcement may request an order of the court declaring the person incompetent so that appropriate new arrangements can be made. This kind of action must be viewed as a last resort, to be used only when all other approaches have failed. And, if it is done, unusual efforts must be made to assure respect for the dignity and well-being of the individual.

The Basics Again

The fundamental emphases with which this chapter began deserve reiteration. Good housing and good location are among the essential ingredients to satisfy deep human needs for *independence, security, identity,* and *well-being.* Adequate and dignified living arrangements, therefore, should be the concern of government at all levels, communities and neighborhood organizations, and certainly the church which responds to its Lord's passion for justice and fullness of life.

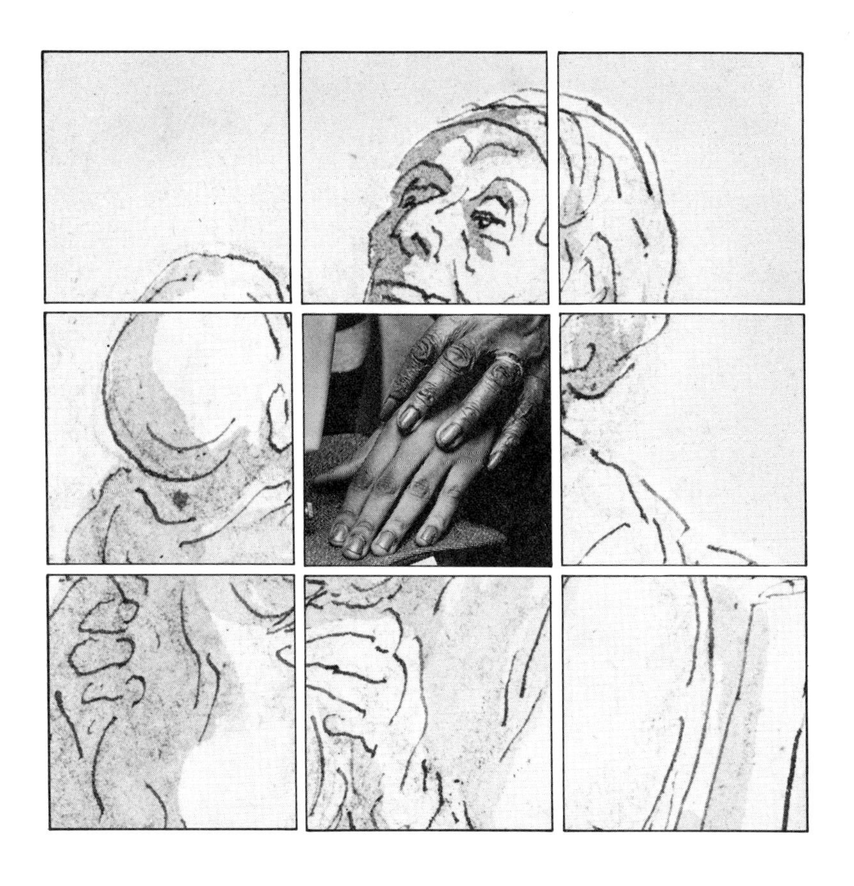

5 Education

Education

According to Robert Butler, of the National Institute on Aging, the average city dweller over 65 has no more than an eighth grade education. In rural areas this average is even lower. The lack of a high school education severely limits job opportunities and is a real handicap in making financial and other provisions for retirement. It also militates against a productive and satisfying old age.

Out of nearly 23 million Americans over 65, more than one-fourth (25.9 percent) have had less than eight years' formal schooling. Their median level of educational attainment, as of the March 1977 Current Population Survey (U.S. Bureau of the Census), was only 9.5 years. Only one-fifth (20.7 percent) had finished four years of high school.

True, the academic attainment of the older segment of the American population will improve through the coming years. The survey just quoted indicates that — compared with the 9.5 median for the present over-65 group — the median schooling completed by those now 35-44 and 45-54 is, respectively, 12.5 and 12.4 years. At the same time, we should not forget that many older people without formal schooling are able to educate themselves and achieve a wisdom, a *savoir faire*, and a joy in life that go far beyond those of many more highly-educated contemporaries.

Many primary and secondary schools can hardly be said to give their pupils the basic tools and skills of the educated person, let alone the full development of particular talents. Overcrowded schools, overworked and underpaid teachers, unfavorable home conditions, and poor health too often make a shambles of public education. Add to these a general anti-intellectual climate, stodgy traditionalism or wild experimentation, rigid discipline or excessive freedom, and bad results are compounded. The many first-rate schools that still do exist cannot obscure the inexcusable conditions rife on the educational scene.

There must be a veritable revolution in public and private education alike if people are to be properly prepared for lifelong living. Consider the vast expansion of knowledge over the past few decades. Changes introduced by the space age alone are said to be greater than those in all the preceding millennia. And who knows how many more startling breakthroughs are about to come?

The past has seen many incomparable discoveries, inventions and advances. We think of language, the alphabet, mathematics and geometry, the wheel, gunpowder, the steam and gasoline engines, electricity, the circulation of the blood, the telescope, the microscope, pasteurization — the list goes on and on. Yet none of these can quite compare in its potential for good and evil with the advent of nuclear power and the opening of space to human exploration.

Each day brings new facts and methodologies that make yesterday's knowledge obsolete. Thus, as Butler points out, many professional or scientific careers may be over by midlife. This is why we see increasing emphasis on continuing education, constant retraining programs, education for more than one career and what Butler calls "life cycle education."

Although Butler is right that our educational system needs radical overhauling, his negativism is exaggerated. It is just not true, as he says, that *no one* tells the child of his unique potentials and prized privileges or that *no one* takes pains to liberate him genuinely. Many marvelous teachers are content, like the Socratic midwife, to help give birth to what is within their pregnant pupils — not least among them the aged, with the wisdom of their years.

At least three types of education involve older adults:

Education For Its Own Sake

The first of these is education for the satisfaction it gives. Persons who no longer want to learn and improve themselves as long as they have the faculties to do so are simply denying their own humanity. Despite this century's vast increase of knowledge, the surface of things unknown has barely been scratched. Yet in addition to this measureless realm there is also the great storehouse of past wisdom.

There was a brief period when the "young Turks" were repudiating the past, determined to make a completely new start on their own. But what could be more foolish than that? Unlike the insects and the animals, we do not by instinct know how to struggle for existence. Instead, we must learn everything from the ground up, building on the accumulated learning of the past. Apart from instinct, the insect is an utter idiot, but man has the flexibility and powers of an almost infinitely complex brain.

This unique and decisive advantage over the beast gives us a limited range of freedom to conquer and subdue the earth or destroy it and ourselves with it. So what could be more fascinating or liberating than the study of history — in spite of the cynic's claim that the only thing we learn from the past is that we learn nothing from the past? The study of the past —its culture, philosophy, religion, social life, art, music, sports — is virtually inexhaustible. Although we should by no means neglect the myths, poetry and dreams human beings have conjured up by the power of their imagination, truth is indeed stranger than fiction. Many today are turning again with avid interest to the past, their own particular past in all its pathos, wonder, joy and tragedy.

Besides, there are so many arts and skills — not just to idle away dull hours pouring innumerable clay ash trays, but really to test one's dexterity and creativity.

The first reason for educating the elderly, or anyone else for that matter, is for the sake of knowing, for the sheer thrill of achievement — not for any ulterior, pragmatic motive. And once the educated person has the basic tools for this pursuit, he or she is set for life.

The National Council on the Aging has developed The Senior Center Humanities Program, which is supported by a grant from the National Endowment for the

Humanities. The program provides eight-week guided sessions in which older adults encounter many of the greatest writers and thinkers. Along with selections from literature, poetry, drama, history and the Bible, groups make visits to community museums, art galleries, historic landmarks and wilderness areas.

Although there has been a great increase in adult education and extension courses since World War II, more are needed. About 40 percent of all colleges now offer courses to adults who are not necessarily working for degrees. A few also offer special degree programs. Some make no charge at all for the elderly, others give reduced rates. Over 200 American educational institutions in 30 states participate in Elderhostel, which offers special low-cost, one week residential academic programs for older persons during the summer months. Unfortunately, most American universities still have age limits for degree candidacy; as Butler points out, we are far behind the so-called Third Age College at France's University of Toulouse, which has over a thousand retired persons as students.

He also stresses the necessity of saving age-old human skills from obsolescence. The aged themselves should become teachers. Butler even suggests that old-age homes should have directors of learning in addition to recreational directors. He quotes Rabbi Abraham Heschel as saying that the nation needs "senior universities" where wise men teach the potentially wise — not to prepare them for a career, but for the sake of learning itself.

The parish has a responsibility to stimulate the thirst for

knowledge in the elderly, and not allow them to give up and vegetate. It can create the right atmosphere of inquiry, sponsor lectures or open a library, and encourage the community to provide educational opportunities.

Education for Retirement

In addition to education for its own sake, there is also education designed to prepare people for retirement long enough ahead of time so that the dread day will not come as a shock and catch them unawares. The following are some general topics that should be a part of planning:

* Cultivation of the proper attitude toward old age and retirement.
* Discussion of the pros and cons of enforced retirement.
* Cooperative planning — involving husband, wife and perhaps other relatives and dependents.
* Financial concerns.
* Housing.
* Health.
* Constructive use of leisure and time in general.

People should be helped to plan for their own futures, instead of just reacting passively to whatever comes along. They should be helped to decide for themselves what they really would like to be and do. Even with limited resources, there are so many possibilities from which to choose that no one should be bored or just doing "busy work."

Education for Social Utilization

This type of education trains people for special skills and keeps them up to date amid rapid social changes.

Factory workers are not the only ones who need constant retraining. The same principle applies to the natural sciences, medicine, engineering, law, teaching, social work, the ministry and countless other fields. It also applies to the elderly — who often need re-education in order to make continuing constructive contributions. For them, such education may embrace totally new fields.

Life Cycle Education

One of Butler's most helpful suggestions is what he calls "life cycle education." Today's social and individual forces tend toward rigidification, he holds, with the result that political, educational, economic, cultural and other constraints need loosening up.

American society organizes people's lives into three broad phases. First comes a solid block of education running into one's twenties, when students are given a "one-chance" shot at learning. It may be something that doesn't really interest them, something they simply drift into and for which they are unfitted. Sometimes they get shoved into niches, square pegs in round holes, and become thoroughly miserable. It might be better if, after an initial period of basic education, they were allowed to work or travel for a while till they found themselves.

Second, there is a central, massive 40-year block of work with little time left over either for further education or for creative leisure. For many Americans, this is the period for sinking into dull conformity and mediocrity — if not vegetation and boredom.

Third comes retirement, when many are too exhausted to enjoy their belated leisure and others are unhappy not to continue working. Still others are too blunted in mind and spirit by the daily grind to know what to do with their time.

What Butler suggests is a radical redistribution of education, work and leisure throughout the life cycle—instead of the present rigid compartmentalization. Rather than being separate and consecutive, these three modes of living should run concurrently and continuously throughout life.

The young should feel free to work or travel as well as attend college. The 40 year-old should be able to take time off for study, a change of direction, or relaxation. And the 70 year-old, because of his diversity of experience, would be well prepared for work, study or leisure. Such a redistribution would help solve the problem of enforced retirement, since the elderly could then substitute in the job force for younger people who are being "retooled" or allowed to enjoy themselves.

Such a system would require changes that no one seems to have worked through. Mid-career clinics, sabbaticals and shorter work weeks are small experiments in the right direction. In many cases, though, shorter work weeks mean moonlighting to make more money. Perhaps Social Security benefits could be used before retirement.

However difficult it may be to work out, Butler's proposal makes admirable sense in view of present unemployment problems, the advance of mechanization and cybernetics, the problems of early retirement of the worker, and the system's tendency to encourage mediocrity. Our great nation needs to reorder its priorities if it is to survive. Life cycle education would most certainly favor freedom of choice for all people, including the elderly, in their ways of living.

Like everyone else, pastors also need to expand skills and develop talents that may not be directly related to their duties. Congregations should therefore give their pastors time off for continuing education and general self-development.

Christian Education

Much of what we have said about education in general also applies to Christian education as a lifelong concern. The old would be better prepared for the trials and opportunities of age if they were properly informed about the Bible and the history, teachings and demands of the church. And they would be better prepared for death.

There is no guarantee, though, that the mere possession of information will vitally affect life-styles. Christianity does not deal with universal truths that can simply be accepted off the top of one's head. Christian faith puts a claim on the faithful that requires a transformation of their existence. The traditional way of saying this is that only the Holy Spirit (God Himself) can lead a person to faith.

Christian education — instruction in and knowledge about the faith of the church — is nevertheless an essential prerequisite for coming to faith. The present state of the church — its uninformed biblicism, its militant fundamentalism, its uncontrolled pentecostalism — is a sad commentary on its educational achievements.

With the number of old people in the church increasing rapidly, their education becomes a matter of priority. It is often said that the elderly are conservative and traditionalist. Why then, we might ask, should they be upset in their accustomed beliefs and practices, if these are not in obvious contradiction to the Christian proclamation? It simply is not proven that the old as a group are resistant to change. Rather, the opposite may be the case. They have run their course. They have nothing to lose. They are not tied to conventions. They are no longer dependent on "the boss" or "what people will think." In a sense they can thumb their noses at the world. They are free for change and experimentation, and for some better ways than the old ways they have seen to fail. They are ready, that is, provided they have been educated for this kind of freedom — the true Christian freedom of which we speak in the chapter on "Christian Perspectives on Aging."

Most old people have time for further Christian education, and the church should offer it to them. They have as much need for it and right to it as young people.

Each congregation should take a look at the educational resources available to its elderly for general as well as Christian education — and then use them more fully and supplement them where necessary. This can be done through synod task forces, a network of advisors to congregations, or "senior staffers" comparable to youth staffers.

The Elderly as Teachers

Old people with the necessary education and experience should themselves be used as teachers. As we have said, many of them are going back to school to prepare for such positions. Others continue to be self-educated and are prepared to teach by a lifetime of Christian experience. The stereotype of the half-senile, prissilly pious old Sunday school teacher who alienates the young should be replaced by the stimulating oldster with a head as well as a heart. There is a place here also for retired pastors, missionaries, and other church workers.

This is one of the main areas where the church should be constructively active. It must not let the great potential of increasing numbers of the elderly go to waste. It is not enough to wait for them to volunteer. Their services should be sought out, and they should be given every encouragement to develop and make use of their talents.

Those Who Work with the Aged

The education of those who work with the aged is a topic broad enough to deserve separate treatment. Its urgency requires emphasis. Of a group of ministers recently surveyed, a majority felt no special training was needed for work with the aged — and this correlated in nearly every instance with the absence of special programs in their own congregations.

Institutions for the aged also report constant streams of volunteers who come without preparation of any kind. Such workers usually begin with high enthusiasm — which rapidly dwindles. They soon find out that they simply don't know how to cope with the variety of people they encounter. One needs primarily to talk and have someone listen. Another is just the opposite: eager to listen, to be talked to, to find out what's going on. Still a third seems completely passive and unresponsive; nothing seems to get through. Yet with persistent, loving attention even apparently senile people have often reawakened, taken renewed interest in the world, and begun to live again. To the degree possible, volunteers, whether they are to work in the congregation, the community, or an institution, should be trained as carefully as employed personnel.

There is much to know about the process of aging — the subject matter of the science of gerontology — about the problems and foibles of the aging as well as their assets and potential.

A survey of a group of church-related colleges revealed that too little is being done to give youth adequate orientation to old age, to counteract the current youth-oriented culture, to prepare them for their own aging, and to involve older people in formal and informal educational programs.

What seminaries are doing also presents a mixed, for the most part pitiful, picture. Certainly more needs to be done. Work with the aged should receive as much attention as work with youth. Ideally, all seminaries should give basic instruction in gerontology, utilizing the resources of academic gerontological centers, which are usually related to universities. Some should specialize in exploring and teaching gerontology in relation to the church. It is a questionable procedure to turn over youth work to the young minister and work with the aged to the older one. Perhaps this custom should be reversed. Concern and training are far more important qualifications than age. It is a matter of using gerontology as an ancillary science — so that the gospel may be properly proclaimed.

Church agencies and institutions working with older people must see to the proper education of their personnel. They should not assume it is enough if people are willing to "work cheap" for the love of Jesus.

This by no means implies that love is not essential. The famous institutions of Pastor von Bodelschwingh in

Bethel-Bielefeld, Germany, and many other lesser known establishments are demonstrating what a combination of Christian consecration and proper training can do for those who need nothing so much as love — love treating them as persons for whom Christ died, each infinitely precious, baptized by name and written into the Book of Life. Love that does not take the form of skilled care is nothing but pious sentiment.

Congregations, then — along with colleges, seminaries, and social service institutions that work with the aged — should all strive for Christian consecration and skilled performance, not pitting one against the other.

A positive approach to education for older adults and those who work with them follows from the clear recognition that men and women normally retain the ability to learn and to think as long as they live, provided they exercise that ability.

6 Community Programs and Services

Community Programs and Services

The overwhelming majority of older adults require no special community provisions to bolster their morale or service their needs. They adjust to the later years much as they have adjusted to the changing patterns of the earlier years. They cherish independence, and that includes independence from outside help as long as possible. Some of the elderly, to be sure, require considerable assistance throughout the older years, and most require certain kinds of support sooner or later. In these situations their families, friends, congregations, and communities must be prepared to assist.

Although this chapter focuses upon the function of the community, the importance of the roles of families, friends, and congregations must also be underscored.

Family and Friends

When people talk about the family in relation to the elderly, they usually think in intergenerational terms. How do adult children behave with regard to their parents, and vice versa? Although these questions must be asked and answered, they tend to obscure the fact that for most older people the spouse is most important. By far the largest number of older men and women are elderly couples living in their own households. Less than ten percent have never married and about two percent are divorced. Extensive surveys have revealed a great deal of happiness among older households. They have also revealed, to be sure, a considerable amount of tension and hostility, with the proportions between these different kinds of atmosphere not far different from younger households.

The important thing to emphasize is that, in a very large number of cases, basic physical and emotional support of an individual in time of need comes from husband or wife.

The research led by Bernice Neugarten, of the University of Illinois, and others also reveals the extended kinship network to be a far more important and reliable source of support than the popular stereotype suggests. This represents, for the most part, a linkage among nuclear families which themselves retain basic autonomy within the network.

Friends are frequently as important as family in the supportive relationships of older persons. A confidant, a person who listens and can be trusted, often enables the man or woman to face adequately most of the problems and losses that accompany aging. The confidant may be either the spouse or someone else. The elderly tend to choose friends of the same age, sex, marital status, and socioeconomic group.

It is essential to remember the large number of older adults who live alone, often with no significant contact with family members and with few friends or group associations. Some of these people, especially if they have lived alone through most of their lives, seem to get along relatively well in old age. But many more live in unrelieved loneliness. These men and women represent a tremendous challenge to communities and churches.

Let's talk about the supportive roles of the community and of the congregation as it functions as part of its community.

The Community

"A community," says Robert C. Atchley, of Miami University in Ohio, "is a group of people who interact with one another frequently, who share their location in space, who depend on one another — even if indirectly — to fill their needs, and who share an identity with the place where they live. Members often share certain ideas that have grown from the unique social heritage of the community. The ideal community is a relatively autonomous locality with a population large enough to foster a full-fledged social system complete with social institutions but small enough to remain integrated.... Most localities have some characteristics of a 'pure' community but few meet the ideal."*

Although communities (including subcommunities in larger areas) are important to most people, they are especially important to older men and women, probably because they have often invested more years and have had more key life experiences there. Since there are differences between communities in cultural values and attitudes, the elderly frequently find it difficult to move. Relocation cuts them off from much that is most meaningful to them.

*Robert C. Atchley, *The Social Forces in Later Life* (Belmont, Calif.: Wadsworth Publishing Co., 1977), p. 261. Reprinted by permission.

Basic Community Facilities

A community includes many facilities which are essential to the lives of its citizens, e.g. stores, banks, churches, doctors' offices, hospitals, schools. In the typical community there is a mixture of public and private facilities. In general, the bigger and more complex an area, the greater the variety of facilities available. Unfortunately, a very large number of communities are limited in such essential services, particularly in rural areas where nearly one-fourth of the older U.S. population lives.

Religious Organizations

A community, furthermore, includes religious organizations and voluntary associations of many kinds. At this point religious organizations are discussed as institutions in the community. Although investigation in this field has not been as extensive as it should or will be, David Moberg, Professor of Sociology at Marquette University, says that research confirms a fact that most of us have long supposed to be the case: that older persons are more involved in churches and synagogues than in all other types of social organizations combined. This is true, Moberg observes, even among the elderly poor, who are not inclined to belong to organizations of any kind. A massive national survey done in 1970 revealed that nearly 60 percent of the respondents, many of whom were poor, named churches and synagogues as the organizations to which they belong. The nearest competitors — fraternal societies — were named by only 5 percent.

There is evidence that internalized religious attitudes, feelings and beliefs become more important with the passing of the years, at least among those to whom they were already important. It may be that older people are not as active participants in church and synagogue worship and program as are some who are younger. To the degree that this is so it is probably because of such factors as physical disability, lack of transportation, economic costs, and a feeling of being left out.

Studies reveal that ministers, priests and rabbis, though quite diligent in visiting older people who are homebound or institutionalized, are slow to recognize and confront the needs of the ambulatory elderly or to encourage the use of their talents. One reason is the lack of specialized training. Another is fear of aging and death, which they share with society as a whole.

Church and synagogue have significant potential to relate to older adults, to minister to their needs, to engage them in ministry to others, and to aid them in developing a vital and enduring philosophy of life. Whether these institutions come even close to realizing this potential is a very serious question.

Voluntary Associations

Nearly every community has a variety of voluntary organizations, which people join or leave of their own free choice. They may include veterans' groups, unions, service clubs, older adults' organizations, and others. Voluntary associations, which generally do not discriminate on the basis of age, can perform many necessary functions for most older people who actually participate in them, e.g., provision for social contacts and personal identification, some structuring of their days, services of one kind or another, and the chance to be where things are going on. However, older persons seem more likely to continue actively in selected voluntary associations if the relationship started during the middle years than to initiate involvement in the later years. And in any case, their degree of participation is influenced by such factors as health, income and availability of transportation.

As with churches and synagogues, voluntary organizations have the ability to offer much greater support and satisfaction to older men and women than they actually provide. Conscious efforts are needed to fulfill their potential.

Social Services

Communities vary widely in the kind and number of social services that are available to older adults. Yet these can be crucial factors in giving people freedom of choice in their way of life.

Some of the services communities can and do provide for older people follow:

Caring visitors. These programs, often staffed by volunteers, including elderly persons themselves, provide contact for shut-ins and the institutionalized with the outside world, and frequently open the door to other important services. One facet of a visitors program may well be *outreach services*, which are planned efforts to find older people in the community who require assistance. Training of workers is necessary.

Telephone reassurance. In this type of program regular telephone calls are made to the homebound to check on their welfare, converse with them, and bring them into contact with any special services they may need. Again, the volunteers who serve may include older persons, among them residents of nursing homes, and training is desirable.

Meal Services. "Meals on Wheels" programs take hot meals to older people (or others who are housebound) in their homes. Congregate meal programs, on the other hand, provide meals to the elderly in group settings. Increasingly other services, such as counseling, information and referral, and educational programs, are made available at the congregate meal sites, which often are church buildings.

Homemaker services. These range from professional to informal programs. Both types are appropriate, since the needs of the semi-independent older people vary a great deal. Homemaker services, on a daily or occasional basis, may include housekeeping, home maintenance, and food preparation. They may be linked with health assistance in the home.

Day care centers. A community can provide facilities under the supervision of appropriate medical or nursing personnel, where older persons, unable to fend for themselves, can receive sensitive and secure care during the day. The arrangement can enable adult children to continue their employment or to obtain some relaxation from responsibility, and it can make the days more interesting for the elderly men and women involved.

Employment services seek to bring together older workers and opportunities for part-time, short-term, or more permanent employment.

Financial counseling helps people make the most of their incomes, buy consumer goods at the lowest prices, buy wisely on credit, form consumer cooperatives, or save on rent, building repairs and insurance. Retired persons knowledgeable in financial matters can participate as counselors.

Health services, mental health centers, addiction clinics. All of these are of great importance to older people, who may have greater need of these facilities than any other segment of the population.

Chore service and minor home repair and maintenance can go far to help older people care for their homes and thus continue to live in them. Personal care, major home improvement projects, etc. would not be included. This program provides opportunity for some older persons to use their skills in performing these services.

Multipurpose senior citizens centers usually take the form of private not-for-profit corporations, often underwritten with funds from the United Way or governmental sources. Although centers offer a good base for the provision of many of the services mentioned in this section, most of them appear to concentrate on recreational and, to a lesser extent, educational activities. For reasons not entirely clear, senior centers attract only one to five percent of the older people within their areas. This has been true even in communities where concerted efforts have been made to overcome the obstacles of inadequate transportation, disability, and poor health. Since many centers are more or less informal groups sponsored by churches, unions and fraternal organizations, it is difficult to secure reliable information about their overall effectiveness or their appeal.

Information and referral services seek to link people who have needs with service agencies that might help meet those needs. There is an appalling lack of knowledge of available services among the general population, including the elderly. Many areas have directories of services for older people, which ought to be publicized far more widely among the churches. Nevertheless, some central source of information and referral is a necessity.

Protective services takes over the affairs of older people who are no longer capable of taking care of themselves. Since there is always danger that relatives or neighbors will over-react and try to have them "put away for their own good," it is essential that these situations be investigated by skilled social caseworkers under the auspices of competent professional agencies. Legal intervention is a possibility, but it should be seen as a last resort to be used only when all other alternatives have been exhausted.

Transportation Services. Transportation is needed by older adults for access to most social services, opportunities for work, recreational facilities, church and synagogue, store and doctor, family and friends. William R. Hutton of the National Council of Senior Citizens stated before a congressional committee: "Being without transportation is like having a modern kitchen with all the latest appliances and no electricity." Because of the dominance of the private automobile, which many older adults cannot afford or are not permitted to drive, and the inadequacies of public transportation in most areas, many of these people become virtual prisoners in their own homes or immediate neighborhoods. A solution can involve social agencies, volunteer programs, special public or private transportation programs, e.g., "Dial-a-Ride," and/or changes in public transit systems which take into consideration the needs of older and disadvantaged people.

Escort service, which is not always related to a structured transportation program, offers person-to-person assistance to the elderly or handicapped who may otherwise refuse to venture out. Escort service can be part of other programs, such as visiting or homemaker services. Escort service should be rendered by intelligent and sensitive people, who relate well to older adults. These workers should also be knowledgeable about community health and social service agencies and about how to help older adults make use of them. In some areas it is important that they be fluent in more than one language. Older persons can be utilized as supervisors, drivers, escorts, and in other capacities in this kind of program.

Not only are there social services for older people; there are also services that are to be rendered by older people. To be sure, the elderly are on the serving end of many of the programs described above. But the following are specifically oriented to giving them the opportunity to assist others.

The Foster Grandparent Program enables low-income older people to help provide personal, individual care to children who live in institutions. The workers receive far more satisfaction than the pay of $40 to $50 per week, but this too is very helpful to them. And the children have shown marked improvement.

The Retired Senior Volunteer Program (RSVP) uses men and women over 60 as volunteers in schools, libraries, hospitals, courts, day care centers, nursing homes, and many other settings. RSVP agencies provide transportation to and from the place of service.

The Service Corps of Retired Executives (SCORE) provides a means whereby retired businessmen and businesswomen help owners of small businesses and managers of community organizations who are having management problems. Volunteers are not paid but they are reimbursed for out-of-pocket expenses.

The Senior Companion Program pays older persons a small stipend to help adults with special needs, such as the handicapped and the disabled.

In addition to these programs, all of which benefit from U.S. Government funds, the Department of Labor has three programs that offer part-time employment to older adults who serve as aides in a variety of community agencies, such as child care centers, vocational training programs, building security, clerical service and homemaker service.

Furthermore, *Green Thumb* is sponsored by the National Farmers Union in 24 states. It provides part-time employment in conservation, beautification, and community improvement in rural areas or in existing community service agencies. The *Senior Aids* program is administered by the National Council of Senior Citizens; *Senior Community Service Aides*, by the National Council on the Aging; and *Senior Community Aids*, by the National Retired Teachers Association/American Association of Retired Persons.

In Canada the federal *New Horizons Program* facilitates activity in the community. Through it grants are offered to groups who undertake activities for themselves and others. As of August 1977 probably a million older persons have been involved directly or indirectly in 7,894 projects. There are programs to give the retired access to educational facilities. In addition, numerous senior citizen centers have been established, with a number of provinces providing funding and consultation. However, such centers are used by a minority of older people.

The success of some of these programs emphasizes the fact that older adults can carry important responsibility, whether their work is voluntary or paid employment. In other facets of community (and church) life, they should be expected to function in significant responsible positions on an ongoing basis, unless the elderly themselves choose not to be thus involved.

Putting It All Together

All of these social services — and others — are very important to older people. But, if they are not effectively coordinated, the intended beneficiaries will be utterly frustrated when they try to use them. To be compelled to visit five different offices for five different services will discourage anybody but an investigative reporter. Yet through the years, calls for better coordination within communities have been largely unheeded.

In 1973, the U.S. Government took a major step forward. The Older Americans Comprehensive Service Amendments of 1973 created a new community organization, the Area Agency on Aging (AAA). This legislation established, through the AAA's, new priorities on coordination of services and on planning. In addition, it significantly increased federal funding of local programs for older Americans. These funds were made available only as states set up AAA's. In each area a single agency was designated as the coordinator of both state and federal programs. There are now several hundred Area Agencies on Aging across the nation, each of which is charged with planning for a comprehensive and coordinated network of services to older people and with facilitating information and referral, escort, transportation, and outreach services.

Although one hears of AAA's that are not doing their job, one hears also of outstanding examples of effectiveness. Since AAA's began comparatively recently, it is still too early to evaluate them adequately.

Many of the services referred to earlier are offered by organizations in the private rather than the public sector. These include programs carried out by churches. In the interest of the well-being of older men and women, these services should be made available in a more coordinated way than has usually been the case. There are many competent professional agencies and institutions sponsored by churches and voluntary organizations. There are also informal, nonprofessional programs which have validity. Yet the overall effectiveness of all of these is too often limited by competition among them and possessiveness on the part of some. Communities should find ways to encourage comprehensive planning and cooperative effort in the private sector, and this coordination should be related to the coordinating functions of the local Area Agency on Aging. This kind of planning is stimulated and guided by NVOILA (National Voluntary Organizations for Independent Living for the Aging), which is related to the National Council on the Aging.

Many of the services mentioned can be offered within the life of a typical congregation. Where a congregation has the necessary strength and commitment there is no reason why this should not be done. A persuasive argument can be made, however, that a congregation will serve older persons better if it presses the community to engage in services on a more comprehensive scale, and then enables its members and those of other churches to participate in these wider programs as volunteers, leaders, and monitors. If all churches and all other organizations do this, the beneficiaries will be *all the elderly* rather than only those who have some identification with those congregations and organizations, and each man or woman has a better chance of being dealt with as a whole person. This emphasis should not prevent a congregation from engaging in informal visiting, telephone reassurance, or other programs which are integral parts of its role as a witnessing, caring fellowship.

A Final Word

We may ask what should be expected of family and friends and what should be expected of the community in relating to older men and women. Although sharp distinctions are impossible, a distinction in primary emphasis might be that family and friends should perform *affective roles,* functioning in the realm of affection, emotions and feelings, and the community should perform *instrumental roles,* concerned with the tasks to be done to advance justice and provide service. The church is closely related to all of these groupings and is itself the community of faith. It should motivate, challenge, and support all elements as they seek well-being for older adults.

7

Finances in the Later Years

Finances in the Later Years

The past decade has seen some significant changes in the economic status of the retired population. Thanks largely to the major social security improvements of 1972, the number of elderly persons below the poverty level fell from approximately 5.4 million in 1967 to 3.4 million in 1973. Since that time, however, thanks largely to the persistently high rates of inflation we have experienced, income improvement has slackened considerably. In 1977, 3.2 million older persons remained below the poverty level, very slight progress since 1973. Income and protection of that income from the effects of inflation have become the economic problem of the retired population, and inflation is likely to remain *the* central economic problem for some time to come.

The purpose of this chapter is to provide the reader with a description of the current economic status of the elderly and the effects of inflation on that economic status. In doing so we hope not only to alert readers to the economic problems of today's retirees but to alert them as well to the problems they may expect to face as they themselves approach retirement age.

Current Income Levels Among the Aged

The Table below presents a number of aspects of the distribution of income among the U.S. population and among the population 65 years of age.

Table I.

Total Money Income[1], Percentages of Families and Persons in Various Income Classes 1976

	Families		Single People	
Income	**all ages**	**65+**	**all ages**	**65+**
Under $4,999	10.3	19.4	43.7	69.7
5,000-7,999	11.7	25.7	18.9	17.3
8,000-9,999	7.9	12.2	9.1	4.5
10,000+	70.1	42.7	24.7	8.5
Median Income	14,958	8,721	5,375	3,495
Average Income	16,870	11,635	7,236	4,886
Number in Class	56,710	8,141	21,459	7,027

[1]Calculated from Money Income and Poverty Status of Families and Persons in the United States, 1976, Series P-60, No-107, September 1977, Table 6, U.S. Bureau of the Census.

As the table shows, older persons' incomes are significantly below those of the rest of the population, with a much greater concentration in the lower and lower middle ranges. The U.S. Department of Labor has calculated a series of budgets or amounts of income necessary to maintain low, intermediate, and high living standards. The amounts necessary in 1976 to achieve these three standards of living were approximately $5,000, $7,000, and $10,000. On the basis of these standards, fully 19 percent of the families headed by persons 65 years of age and 70 percent of the single people in this age group had incomes sufficient to maintain only a "low" standard of living. Although our nation has made some progress in moving older people above the rock-bottom poverty line, it should be quite clear that we have not approached solving the problem of adequate income in retirement, particularly among the single elderly.

Elderly Expenditures

As the previous section indicates, the income of the elderly is significantly lower than that of the average in the U.S. population and, for a very large number of people, barely sufficient. It is useful to consider as well the differences in the way the elderly dispose of this income relative to the rest of the population—the shares of their income which go to various categories of consumer goods.

Intuitively, we might expect that the expenditure patterns of older persons would be significantly different from the patterns of the younger population. In the first place, expenditures which are sensitive to income changes are likely to be reduced, given the pronounced change in income that occurs with retirement.

Second, changes in life-style associated with retirement might be expected to change expenditure patterns. Since, for example, the trip to work is no longer required, reductions in transportation outlays might be expected.

Finally, some outlays are strictly a function of age. For example, medical care expenditures might be expected to be greater for older persons than for the general population. Table II shows expenditures as a percentage of total consumption for both 1960-1961 and 1973 and certainly bears out these expectations.

Table II.

Relative Importance of Expenditures for Selected Goods and Services

	1960-1961[1]		1973[2]	
	Wage and Clerical Workers	Retirees	All Consumer Units	Units with Head 65+
Food				
At home	20.1	22.6	17.0	21.2
Away from home	5.1	3.8	2.2	1.5
Housing				
Shelter	13.2	16.8	16.2	15.8
Fuel	6.0	6.6	5.3	7.4
Furnishings and Operations	9.1	10.5	9.0	9.5
Apparel	10.7	6.8	8.3	6.4
Transportation	14.7	11.0	20.3	14.9
Medical Care	6.2	10.2	6.1	10.2
Reading, Recreation	5.6	3.9	10.2	8.1
Miscellaneous	9.3	7.8	5.4	5.0

Notes: Expenditures as a percentage of total consumption outlays.

[1]Norwood, Cost-of-Living Escalation of Pensions, A Monthly Labor Review Reprint, U.S. Department of Labor Bureau of Labor Statistics, June, 1972, page 21.

[2]Calculated from expenditures data, pages 44 through 53, 1972-1973. Survey of Consumer Expenditures.

In both periods, older persons are observed to spend a larger percentage of their budgets on food (particularly food at home), furnishings and household operations, fuel and utilities, and medical care, while spending less for transportation, apparel, reading, recreation, and education. Of particular interest are the categories of transportation and medical care.

Almost 15 percent of the older family's consumption budget is spent for transportation, even though the trip to work is for most older persons no longer a part of outlays. Of much greater significance, both for purposes of this chapter and for other areas of social policy as well, the share of the budget devoted to medical care is unchanged in spite of the introduction of Medicare. Older persons still spend about 10.2 percent of their budgets on this particular category of goods and services.

These differences become extremely important when appraising the effect of the rate of inflation on older persons because the Consumer Price Index, the mechanism we use to measure price changes, is based on the expenditure patterns of all consumer units. Hence any given price increase for food, fuel or medical care, for example, makes a much greater impact on the elderly population than on the average consumer. These three components absorb 25 percent, 40 percent and 70 percent *more* of elderly household budgets than is the case for the average consumer household.

Social Security

The cornerstone of elderly income security in the United States is the Social Security system. In September 1978 the system was paying an average benefit to retired workers of $262 per month to an estimated 18 million persons. Benefits are also paid to the spouses of retired workers, averaging in that month $132. Annual income amounts from this primary source total $4,728 for "average" married couples and $3,144 for "average" retired individuals, making it quite clear that Social Security provides only a part of the income required in retirement to maintain a reasonable living standard.

The Social Security system offers a worker two options. A worker may wait until he or she reaches age 65 and receive the full benefit to which he or she is entitled, or the worker can accept the early retirement option, taking benefits at age 62. Choosing this latter option involves accepting significantly reduced benefits, however, for the remainder of the worker's lifetime. For example, if a worker was entitled to a monthly benefit of $200 at age 65, the entitlement at age 62 is only $173—about $27 a month less for the rest of the retiree's life. It should be pointed out that the increases a retiree receives in the monthly check if he or she elects to retire some time *after* age 65 are not as great as the loss suffered for retiring early. If the above retiree chooses to retire at age 67, her or his benefit would be approximately $212, a gain of only $12 per month. Hence, the penalty for drawing benefits for two extra years is more than twice as great as the reward for staying in the workforce and drawing benefits for a shorter period of time, hardly an incentive for continued labor force participation.

One of the most controversial provisions of the Social Security system is the so-called retirement test. Upon reaching age 62, one can apply for Social Security benefits, as mentioned above, but receipt of these benefits is contingent upon the older person not earning "too much", else he or she will not be defined as "retired." If the retiree is 62 to 64 years old, "too much" is anything earned over $3,480. From age 65 to 71, the amount is $4,500. After age

72 no earnings test is applied. Once earnings exceed these two points, however, $3,480 for persons 62 to 64 and $4,500 for persons 65 to 71, benefits are reduced by 50 cents for every dollar earned, equivalent to a tax on earnings of 50 percent!

In order to see this more clearly, consider a 65-year old person earning $6,000 a year or $500 a month. In order to qualify for Medicare he applies for his Social Security entitlement. Medicare eligibility is unrelated to earnings and depends solely on the applicant's age. Not so with Social Security benefits. Suppose the applicant's earnings record and work history would qualify him for benefits of $200 a month. The Social Security System disregards the first $4,500 of earnings or $375 a month while the applicant earns $500 a month. Hence, each month he earns $125 "too much," and must pay a penalty by having his benefits reduced by 50 cents for each of these "excess" dollars or $62.50 a month. This leaves him eligible for benefits of only $137.50 a month unless he cuts back on his earnings. If he earned only $4,500 a year he could get his full benefit of $200 a month and have an annual income of $6,900. Because he earns $6,000 a year his benefits are reduced to $137.50 and his annual income is $7,650. By working and earning this extra $1,500 he is only $750 ahead of the situation in which he doesn't work at all! He has been "taxed" because of his work effort at the rate of 50 percent. *This provision is little known among people who are not yet retired, and is critically important for those persons who plan to supplement their retirement income with a part-time job.* Clearly, this provision is a powerful disincentive to continued employment. It should also be kept in mind that earnings are subject also to both the regular income tax and Social Security taxes. Hence, if a Social Security recipient works and earns income beyond the limits specified above, his income is subject to a tax of 70 percent or more, not a very attractive prospect.

One of the most popular and important provisions of the system, particularly when compared to private pensions, is that which provides for an automatic cost-of-living increase in Social Security benefits, compensation for losses suffered because of inflation. Each year a calculation is made as to how much prices have increased over the year and adjustments are made to the retiree's monthly check. Generally speaking, these adjustments have served as a partial defense against the eroding effects of inflation on Social Security benefits. It is important to note, however, that there are two shortcomings to the automatic adjustment process. First, there is a long delay before checks are actually adjusted for inflation losses. If, for example, prices increased by 8 percent during the course of this year, it will be *July of next year* before Social Security checks are actually increased. Although the Social Security system does compensate retirees for inflation losses, it does so only after quite a long lag. Secondly, these adjustments are based on the Consumer Price Index, which, as discussed earlier, is an index number constructed for the "average consumer." As we all know, how badly we are hurt by inflation depends upon how much prices increase for the things *we* buy, not what happens to the "average" consumer. Since we know retirees spend their money quite differently from the "average consumer," spending much more of their incomes on medical care, food and utilities, it is quite likely that an index based on how the average consumer spends his income will not accurately reflect the price experiences of the older population. Hence, while we might find that prices have increased by 8 percent for the average consumer, they may have increased by 10 percent for the older person. There is some evidence that the Consumer Price Index does indeed understate the effect of inflation on older people, and that the Social Security adjustment based on this average Consumer Price Index is undercompensating them for losses actually suffered by inflation. At the moment this matter is under consideration by the Congress. Attempts are being made to introduce an Elderly Consumer Price Index such as exists in England.

Older women have special income problems, which are largely the result of two factors.

First, continuing discrimination against women in hiring and pay scales results in lower lifetime earnings and lower retirement income for women who are self supporting.

Second, retirement income systems, both public and private, have failed to respond to the changing status of women in society, Such systems tend to assume that women will fall into one of two clearcut categories — either totally self-supporting or totally dependent — throughout their adult lives. It is more likely, however, that women of today will move from time to time from one category to the other. Furthermore, in a large number of families both husband and wife are employed.

Under Social Security, for example, a working wife who has reached retirement age is eligible for benefits which she has earned or for benefits to which she is entitled from her husband's earnings, whichever is higher. She does not receive both. This means that, if her own earnings were too low to result in a larger benefit, she receives no more than if she had never worked and not paid any Social Security taxes.

In addition, serious questions are being raised about the lack of Social Security coverage of certain jobs held mainly by women, most notably those of housewife and mother. Is it possible, is it advisable, for the Social Security system to assign monetary value to the woman's contribution to the family, in such a way that she may receive benefits in her own right at retirement?

In summary, the Social Security system has done more for the alleviation of poverty among the elderly and the provision of income security for retirees than any other social program in the United States. It is not, however, perfect. The increases in monthly benefits for continued work are not fair, the earnings test severely limits older persons in their attempts to supplement Social Security income with earnings, the system provides only a partial defense against the effects of inflation, and there are special income problems for women. These facts provide some of the explanation for early retirement. Any system that includes disincentives to labor force participation is encouraging early retirements. It is, nevertheless, clear why knowledgeable observers regard the Social Security system as such a superb investment for the working population: it is the only major source of income for retired persons in which an attempt is made to protect them automatically against the rate of inflation.

The Supplemental Security Income Program

This program, SSI for short, is specifically designed for

retirees with the lowest incomes. As we know, Social Security benefits are based on the worker's earning record over a lifetime. In cases where persons have suffered extended periods of unemployment or worked at very low paying jobs over their lifetimes, Social Security benefits computed on their earning records can be quite low indeed. The SSI program guarantees a minimum floor of income to persons 65 or older, paying a supplemental amount to Social Security recipients sufficient to bring their incomes up to approximately $190 a month if single and $284 a month if married. Like Social Security benefits, these payments are automatically adjusted for erosion in value due to inflation.

Employment of Older Persons

It is not widely known that elderly labor force participation, in spite of a number of disincentives, is quite significant and that the role of earned income is very important to retired persons' income security. Approximately 35 percent of today's Social Security recipients either do some work over the course of a year or are married to recipients who do. In brief, what goes on in the general economy with respect to employment does matter to a substantial number of the elderly. They are no more insulated against the effects of recession because they are "retired" than they are fully protected from inflation simply because there is a cost-of-living adjustment mechanism included in Social Security.

However, age discrimination and a number of other factors make it difficult for older adults to find employment. It has been estimated that among males under 55 years of age there are 4 persons who no longer bother to even look for work (because they have become discouraged) for every person we actually count as unemployed. But among males 55 or older there are 37 discouraged workers for every person counted as unemployed. We have already mentioned the powerful disincentive to work caused by the workings of the Social Security retirement test. But perhaps the most powerful disincentive is the labor market itself. It should be clearly understood by pre-retirees that there is a great deal of age discrimination in the labor market, that it is difficult for older workers to find employment, and that any retirement income plans that include earned income should be made in light of this fact.

It should also be understood that, generally, part-time workers and particularly elderly part-time workers are not as able as full-time workers to secure inflation adjustments in their wages.

There is only one government program that is specifically designed to help older workers with their employment problems. This is the Senior Community Service Employment Program, a program designed to both provide jobs directly to older people and also to help them find work with private employers. The program is limited, however, to persons 55 years of age or older who are *also* below the poverty level, $2,906 for older individuals and $3,666 for older couples in 1977. These poverty levels are quite low. Furthermore, in 1977 there were only 50,000 jobs available through this program, at a time when the elderly poverty population comprised over 3 million persons. Hence, at least to date, governmental response to the problems encountered by older workers has consisted primarily of a law that outlaws age discrimination and a fairly small employment program to help those who are in desperate economic circumstances.

Other Sources of Income

Approximately 7 million older persons currently receive benefits from private pension plans, benefits estimated to average $195 per month. What is of critical importance with respect to private pensions is the fact that only 4 percent of the plans in the United States provide automatic adjustments to the pensioners' checks for inflation losses. The rest either provide increases only when their current business permits them, or they offer no adjustment at all. At today's rates of inflation it is quite clear that the purchasing power of a pension check declines very rapidly. Given a 9 percent inflation rate, for example, the value of the monthly check is cut in half in just eight years. Given that the average 65 year old man can expect to live 13 more years and a woman even longer, it is very important that *pre-retirees* check into their pension plans to see what provisions, if any, are included to protect their pensions from the effects of inflation. Once retirement occurs, there is very little a retiree can do to alter the terms of a pension plan.

Savings represent a major source of income for retired persons, but this is an income source that is very vulnerable to the eroding effects of inflation. The federal government, through a mechanism called Regulation Q, sets the interest rates banks may pay on savings accounts. Today, with an inflation rate in excess of 9 percent, the government is permitting financial institutions to pay only 5¼-5½ percent interest a year. Very simply, without allowing for compounding, a person who puts $1,000 into a savings account at the beginning of the year will have at the end of that year only $960 in purchasing power, even including interest! Unless the federal government permits interest *payable* to savers to rise with market forces, passbook savings accounts will continue to be relatively poor investments for the average saver. We should also point out that Government Savings Bonds available to small savers are not significantly better investments. Unless a saver has a rather large amount of money, $10,000 or above, there are almost no savings plans available that protect her or him against inflation. Although there have been numerous proposals to change Regulation Q and a great deal of debate concerning the low interest rates available to small savers, at present it appears likely inflation will continue to erode the value of savings.

Inflation Protection

It is clear that inflation represents the greatest threat to a reasonable standard of living in retirement. In spite of government efforts to contain it, it is likely to remain so in the future. Realistically, there are few things to suggest beyond the obvious that an individual can do to attempt to protect himself. In a word, all suggestions fall under the category of pre-planning. While still in the pre-retirement years individuals must attempt to calculate what their retirement income and expenses will be and what aspects of this calculation will be particularly vulnerable to inflation. Does the company pension plan provide inflation adjustments? If so, does it give a full cost-of-living increase, or is it "capped," e.g. limited to no more than 3 percent? How often will these adjustments be made? What interest rate does the bank pay on savings? Are there any alternatives available that would better protect savings from inflation? For example, many stock brokerage houses offer "money market funds," which invest only in 100 percent safe U.S. Government securities, paying 8, 9 or 10 percent a year. These funds, available to anyone with as little as $1,000 to invest, represent a clear improvement over savings accounts for inflation protection. Suggestions have been made that pre-retirees cut back on their spending prior to retirement not only for the obvious purpose of increasing savings but also to cushion the impact from the reduced income and life-style changes that will be forced at retirement. Other suggestions involve the pre-purchasing of high quality durable goods like cars and various items for home improvements prior to the retirement years to avoid these expenditures while in retirement. It should also be pointed out that credit becomes increasingly difficult to obtain in later years, perhaps another reason for undertaking these expenditures in advance of retirement.

As important as planning for retirement is, a significant governmental response will be required to really make the changes required to protect retirees from inflation. In the Social Security area at least three major changes are called for. First, the measurement of inflation's impact should be done with a retirees' price index. Secondly, adjustments must be made more frequently than once a year — at a minimum, twice a year. Finally, the Social Security retirement test must be eliminated, to permit older people who must supplement their living standards with a job the freedom to do so without financial loss.

Another major area for governmental response is in the elimination of Regulation Q and the development of new savings instruments. The elimination of Regulation Q would be a step in the direction of making today's high interest rates available to small as well as large savers. The government should consider the creation of a new savings bond, one that promises savers an "after-inflation" interest rate —something today's bonds do not do. Such a "retirement bond" would do much to encourage people of all ages to prepare for their own retirement. Only if financial changes such as these come into effect will retirees' savings be offered protection against inflation.

Although the government cannot mandate private pension cost-of-living adjustments, it could provide preferential tax treatment for firms that do. It will remain, however, the individual's primary responsibility to find out just how his pension plan works and to try to change provisions that are not satisfactory.

Finally, the best protection against inflation is a job. Delayed retirements mean more years of higher incomes, more years of savings, and fewer years of living on relatively fixed incomes. Retirement should be a matter of choice. If people choose to retire at 55 or at 75, so be it, but the government should try to remain neutral in the matter. Delayed retirement should bring actuarily fair increases in Social Security benefits. Further the government should insure that older persons get a fair share of public service employment jobs under the Comprehensive Employment and Training Act (CETA), and that manpower training programs for older workers are significantly expanded. The Senior Community Service Employment Program should be substantially expanded beyond its current enrollment of 50,000. The need for employment and the SCSEP program's ability to handle expanded enrollment easily justify an expansion by an additional 50,000 openings.

Summary

The inflation we have experienced over the course of the past five years is threatening to erode badly the economic progress and improvement in living standards experienced by older people in the early part of this decade. The Social Security system and the Supplemental Security Income program remain the most important aspects of elderly economic welfare, primarily because these programs offer a great deal of inflation protection to older adults. Private pensions rarely provide inflation protection and government regulation has prevented small savers from reaping the benefits of the very high interest rates of recent times. Finally, income supplementation from part-time employment is severely limited by the Social Security earnings limitation and the existence of age discrimination in the job market. All things considered, it seems obvious that the elderly and the retired will remain first among the groups most severely harmed by high and persistent rates of inflation, and that our major social objective of providing income adequacy for our retired population will continue to be extremely difficult to attain.

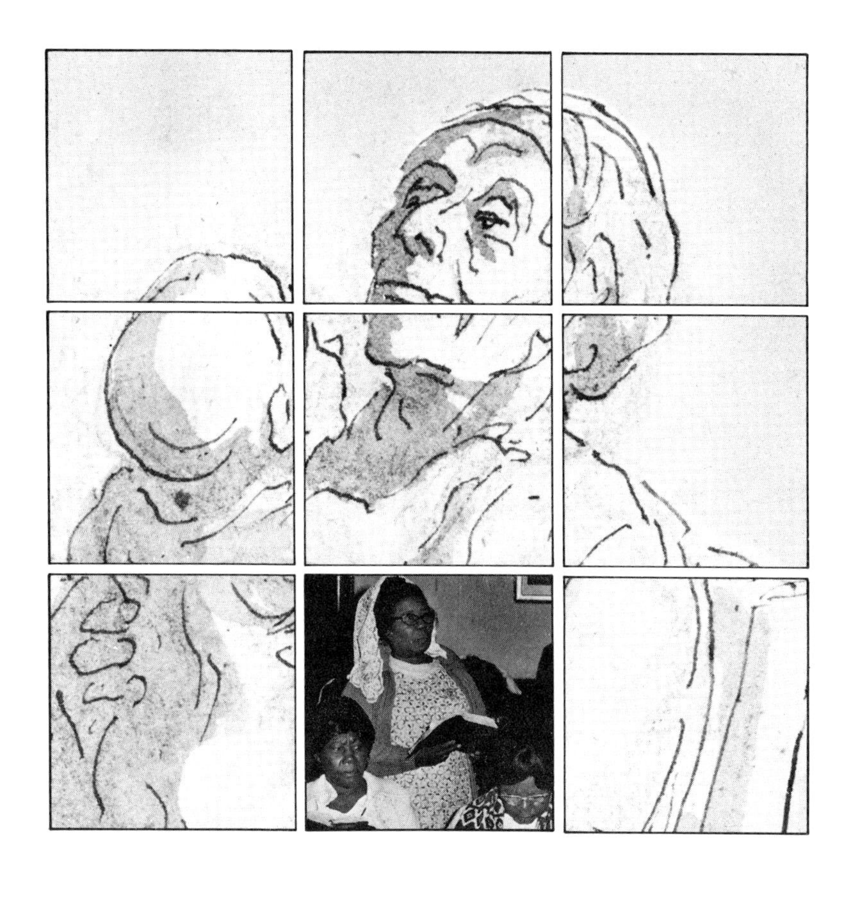

8 Word and Sacrament: The Ground of the Church's Ministry

Word and Sacrament: The Ground of the Church's Ministry

The later years of Mr. Gray bring out some of the characteristics of the church's ministry to an older Christian person — a ministry which is grounded in the Word and the sacraments.

Baptized in the church, Mr. Gray's whole life was centered in the fellowship of the church gathered around the means of grace. His response was lived out through his roles as husband and father, through his occupation, and through his church school teaching and his service to his neighbors in the community.

Upon retirement Mr. Gray gave large amounts of time to special services as a congregational visitor to shut-ins and as a member of various committees. When he was 73 years old a leg problem forced him to use a cane, and a heart condition restricted him to a minimal amount of physical exertion. He was still able to attend services of worship and meetings at the church, thanks to a gift of the women's organization several years earlier that had made possible the construction of ramps and a chair lift at the church building.

During Mr. Gray's later years the church ministered to

him through periods of adjustment to the loss of his wife, retirement, the death of a daughter, increased physical limitations, and the approach of his own death at age 82. Throughout his life this conscientious Christian had ministered to others in response to the gospel. He continued this ministry during his last nine years, even as he became increasingly the recipient of counseling and care administered by others.

Approximately two years before his death, Mr. Gray was confronted with several choices: remaining in his apartment with the aid of someone preparing his meals; leaving his lifelong friends to live with a daughter in the South with whom he had a good relationship; moving to the home of a son in the area with whom he did not relate well; or entering a nearby church home for the aged. During the course of frequent conversations in Mr. Gray's home, as well as a visit together to the church home, the pastor assisted his parishioner through the experience of grief at giving up so much that he cherished, and helped him make the necessary decisions. Following is a summary of a key conversation:

Pastor: "It is a very hard decision to make, but you know what the difficulties will be whichever way you decide."

Mr. Gray: I think going into the home will be the best thing. I'll see my doctor tomorrow about filling out the forms."

Pastor: "This change will not be easy, but I know God will provide the strength that you need...."

Mr. Gray: (smiling) "What's that in the Bible? There's a time for everything. Something about a time to plant and a time to pull up what is planted. How's it go?"

Pastor: "A time to plant and a time to pull up what is planted. A time to build up and a time to break down. A time to keep and a time to let go... something like that. I can't think of it all, the exact words."

Mr Gray: I've had to make a lot of adjustments and changes in recent years. They have all had new rewards I didn't see at the time."

Mr. Gray became a resident of the church home. Even as he added new friends there, he continued his friendships in this church and community. Two years after his entrance into the home, Mr. Gray's health rapidly declined. A few days before his death the congregation had communion. The pastor visited Mr. Gray and asked if he would like to receive the sacrament. "Yes, very much," replied Mr. Gray, "I don't have too much time left, the doctor tells me."

Mr. Gray shared with the pastor his regret concerning the poor relationship he had had with his son. He recounted his years of marriage and involvement in the church. He accepted his own impending death and whatever days remained for him. The pastor, remembering Mr. Gray's bringing up Ecclesiastes 3 during the visit two years earlier when the decision had been made to enter the home, offered to read that passage again. As they read verses 1 through 11b, the pastor kept thinking of Mr. Gray's active, meaningful, and often difficult life. The concluding verse had spoken to the pastor himself, and he hoped it would speak to his friend also: "He has made everything beautiful in its time."

Mr. Gray then received the Sacrament of the Altar with the traditional words of assurance, confession, and absolution, the Words of Institution and the Prayer of Thanksgiving, thanking God for His presence and committing himself to God's love and care. As the pastor left, Mr. Gray appeared pleased and relaxed, and at peace. Three days later Mr. Gray died.

Mr. Gray's life had revolved around the means of grace. Through Word and sacraments he had been nurtured and strengthened to serve his neighbor. The Word and the sacraments had also enabled his pastor and fellow Christians to counsel him through various crises and, at times, simply to be with him in pastoral care and support. That support prevented the kind of "death" that comes from isolation and loneliness. Mr. Gray had made a choice in living which confirmed his incorporation into the community of faith and made his life a choice even unto death. Our faith affirms that not even death has separated Mr. Gray from the love of God in Jesus Christ.

The church's ministry today is widely diversified. It reaches out to persons of all ages who have needs that are personal, spiritual, social, economic. Yet the ministry of the church, while far from having one focus, finds its unique basis in the Word and the sacraments. They are the means of God's grace through which the message of God's unconditional love, the forgiveness of sins, and the "glorious liberty of the children of God" are given to all persons (Romans 8:21).

The Worshiping Community

In the worshiping community the Holy Spirit gathers Christians around the means of grace. It is here that all believers, whatever their ages, are nurtured and strengthened in God's love. Paul's analogy of the church as a body is expressed in a congregation, where the means of grace touch persons of all ages in ways significant for their particular needs. For example, in a congregation the older members should be attentive to and supportive of children's sermons, youth folk choirs and special youth observances, while the youth should be attentive to and supportive of worship experiences that appeal to those who are older.

Since the means of grace — the Word and the sacraments — are the ground of the church's ministry, special efforts must be made to include in the worshiping fellowship aging members whose participation is limited by difficulties with hearing, seeing or moving about. Some suggestions:

* amplification and hearing aid devices in the nave and in rooms used for education and fellowship;
* scripture, service books and devotional material available in braille, large print, or on audio equipment;
* ramps, railings, non-skid floor coverings, chair lifts, elevators, etc. to facilitate free movement by the handicapped; and
* regular administration of the Lord's Supper in homes, hospitals and nursing facilities to members who desire it.

Sent Out for Ministry

From this focus in Word and sacrament the church is sent out in ministry. As its members have received the forgiveness of sins, peace with God and life eternal, the Spirit sends them forth. This ministry is grounded in that of Christ himself. "As the Father has sent me, even so I send you" (John 20:21). It is defined by Christ in many places in Scripture: "I came that they may have life and have it abundantly" (John 10:10). "The Spirit of the Lord is upon me, because he has anointed me to preach good news to the poor. He has sent me to proclaim release to the captives and recovering of sight to the blind, to set at liberty those who are oppressed, to proclaim the acceptable year of the Lord" (Luke 4:18-19).

The gifts that are given by the Spirit to the church are of great variety. No single part of the body of the church, according to Paul, can claim superiority and no Christian is equipped with all the gifts (I Corinthians 12). All parts of the body are encouraged to foster mutuality and interdependence in ministry across the generations. All ages are called to minister with their special gifts, but the one gift that belongs to all is the gift of love (I Corinthians 13).

The Ordained Pastor

Ministry belongs to all Christians with their unique and interdependent gifts. All arc members of a "royal priesthood"(I Peter 2:9). The ordained ministry, the official representative ministry of the church, has a particular responsibility to equip the saints, to enable all believers to engage in ministry.

Nevertheless, pastors also have their own direct roles in counseling and ministry to people. Studies have shown that the person called upon most frequently when problems or crises arise is the ordained pastor. One study, by J. Paul Brown, "estimated that 29 percent of people suffering from emotional problems turn to their physicians, while 42 percent seek their minister." The very nature of the pastor's work brings him or her into contact with the largest group of people encountered by any single profession. With an understanding of the specific needs and emotional problems of the aging, the pastor can render a most valuable service in her or his own ministry and in training lay persons for such ministries. Surprisingly, however, David Moberg, of Marquette University, reports that of 109 clergymen belonging to eleven ministerial associations in the Milwaukee area, only 29 percent "had any specific preparation to help them understand experiences and feelings of people as they grow older, and still fewer felt their preparation was adequate."

Moberg and others, including Butler, point out that even among professionals, gerontophobia (fear of one's own aging), ageism (stereotyping of older persons), and personal relationships with parents are all factors impeding proper ministry with the aging. If the Milwaukee experience is at all typical, those most often called upon to give leadership in the church are in dire need of assistance in this area of ministry. Local congregations need to encourage their pastors to seek the training necessary to assist them and lay members to become more effective in ministry to and with older persons.

Counseling of Older Adults

The church's ministry through the gift of counseling can help provide freedom for the aging in choosing their way of life. It is one thing for older adults to have choices available as a result of legislative action making possible more adequate income, housing, medical care, lifelong education and other essentials, but quite another thing for the aging to take advantage of the opportunities that exist in their communities. A great deal of the knowledge we have is like gasoline in the tank that cannot find its way into the engine.

A large number of older persons have the economic resources and the physical and mental capacities to make necessary decisions. For others, however, who have experienced physical and/or psychological losses or whose economic situations limit their freedom of decision, skilled counseling can help them make choices that will increase their fulfillment in living. All persons associated with older adults, be they friends or family members, should be aware of some of the obstacles to their freedom of choice in ways of living.

In ministering with persons at any stage of life, the counselor, whether clergyman, social worker or doctor, encounters resistance. Counseling with the aging, however, often presents peculiar difficulties. Older age is the stage of growth that is generally resisted more than any other. Although all stages of life involve experiences of loss and impoverishment, the later years are the time in which losses occur more rapidly and in which they are interpreted to mean the approaching end of life. "The longer one lives (as the longer one gambles)," someone has written, "the more regularly one loses." One's resources, energies, adaptability, and relationships with family and friends are diminished more and more. It becomes increasingly difficult to transcend or find substitutes for limitations and losses. This situation is bound to appear as a threat to personhood. Consequently, the individuals who most need counseling are those who try to avoid confronting their limitations or exploring the possibilities open to them for service and new choices in living.

Behavior of older adults that is perceived as negative may actually represent normal phases of grief and depression. If dealt with properly, these experiences can lead persons to healthy adjustments and thus to viable choices in living; but, if poorly handled, they can curtail options at least four ways:

First, the older man or woman may deny to self and / or to others that losses have occurred or that a particular problem exists. Acknowledgment that counseling is needed for a problem is seen as a further attack upon the struggle to remain independent. Yet, this very drive for independence could be an expression of an unrealistic and unhealthful self-centeredness.

Second, the aging person may display anger and protest. "Why does this have to happen to me?" Since the elderly need all the strength possible in the face of increasing losses, they cannot afford to direct the anger at themselves. Their self-interest and desire for protection often lead to subconscious self-punishment or to blaming those closest to them for their difficulties. Loved ones, friends, God, or the pastor (as representing God in some persons' minds) can become the target. Not able to handle the guilt arising from such negative feelings, the aging may then try to atone by making bizarre estate decisions, by increasing self-suffering through the intentional or unintentional development of further physical limitations or by engaging in self-sacrificing behaviors, such as practicing innumerable good works. If friends and professionals involved in ministry do not understand this kind of hostility (which may appear as generosity), the result can be either withdrawal from the older person or support of what looks like exemplary behavior but actually is emotional bondage.

Third, the older adult may respond by withdrawing from other people, since closeness to others continues to make the person vulnerable to losses. He or she may also withdraw from the present into the past. This, Butler stresses, is not to be confused with the "life review" in which the aging like to retell their life story, a process which is often interpreted by ministers, lay and ordained, as a waste of precious time. Such recounting of one's life assists the elderly to put their lives in perspective, and, in the words of Erik Erikson, to "accept their one and only life cycle (with resulting feelings of self-respect, dignity, and integrity) to the degree that integrity is the result." The older person may also withdraw from the present by becoming future-oriented, putting off today's decisions or enjoyments to some imagined future. All such behavior moves the aging away from reality, and sets the stage for inner fantasies and possible senile regression. As such withdrawal progresses choices become increasingly difficult if not impossible.

Fourth, the aging may react by becoming overly helpless and dependent. While a certain degree of dependency is needed in the process of any counseling, excessive dependency can create new complications. If such helplessness persists, the individual's image of self becomes one of dependency, and efforts to assist such a person in making decisions about living style and self-care will become more difficult.

Helping older people to acknowledge and express their feelings concerning loss is a process which frees them to perceive and act upon choices pertaining to their mode of living. Such a process can assist them to place new emphasis upon the quality of life rather than upon quantity of possessions and activities which may have been their preoccupation during their production-oriented years.

Counseling in the Christian context enables the older man or woman (or any other) to realize in life what Martin Luther meant when he said: "A Christian is a perfectly free lord of all, subject to none. A Christian is a perfectly dutiful servant of all, subject to all." This kind of freedom is closely linked with destiny. As Paul Tillich states it, "Destiny is not a strange power which determines what shall happen to me. It is myself as given, formed by nature, history and myself. My destiny is the basis of my freedom, my freedom participates in shaping my destiny." When the losses or limitations that restrict one's style of life are accepted as part of destiny, then one is truly free.

The local congregation's library should have available to parishioners books on counseling and resources to assist them in making personal choices. This collection should include information about medical facilities in the community, about social services such as Meals-on-Wheels and handyman assistance, and about retirement centers and extended care and nursing facilities, with information as to costs, waiting periods, etc., for all such programs.

Pastoral Care

Pastoral care and counseling are not identical. Only a few in any given congregation may possess the special skills required for counseling. Some of the older persons who seek good counseling will not be able to accept their limitations and make appropriate changes in their ways of living. Others will refuse any assistance in making decisions. Still others will be difficult to help because they prefer to remain dependent rather than try to transcend their limitations and redirect their lives. Ordained and lay ministers, therefore, should not lose sight of the fact that visitation of the elderly brings these men and women the assurance of God's love and acceptance, even though they may not be able totally to accept themselves. This ministering cannot properly be called counseling, but it is essential pastoral care and support.

The gift of ministry, which has its basis in the Word and the sacraments, is not solely the prerogative of the ordained clergy. The church is the fellowship of faith, the community of those who in baptism are called to witness and service. The congregation, therefore, should encourage its members to minister to the older adults whose choices have decreased. These older persons may be within the fellowship of the church; or they may be in institutions or other housing in the vicinity of the church.

Persons who participate in ministry with older persons should be given the best possible training. They should be helped to understand that, along with the limitations that often accompany aging,the elderly may also be conscious of new freedoms — the opportunity to do and say what they think, and to go at their own pace, relieved of some of the obligations to jobs and children. Lay and ordained ministers can go far toward meeting such basic human needs as the following, from the Rev. Thomas F. Kennedy, Chaplain, A. Holly Patterson Home, Uniondale, N.Y.:

* Need for affection, friendship and recognition as individuals.
* Need for reassurance, understanding and a sense of belonging.
* Need for a sense of basic self-esteem and personal worth.
* Need for a sense of forgiveness and assistance in handling various guilts and other negative feelings.
* Need for a sense of meaning, purpose and "summing up" of life.
* Need for a hopeful future.
* Need for assistance in making transitions and adjusting to institutional life.
* Need for assistance in coping with physical and mental changes.
* Need for assistance in handling personal crisis situations.
* Need for assistance in handling bereavement and feelings of grief and loss.
* Need for participation in meaningful group experiences.
* Need for a sense of independence, self-control and self-direction.
* Need to give affection and to give self in service and creativity.
* Need for continuing growth, mentally and spiritually.
* Need for assistance in developing appropriate patterns of self-advocacy.
* Need for continuing contact with the religious community outside the institution.

The Congregation as Community

Lest the impression be given that the local congregation

is simply a setting within which individuals — whether clergy or laity — perform acts of service, we must also underscore the congregation's role as the community of faith. The church as a corporate fellowship has unique *potential* to relate to older adults, to minister to their needs, and to engage them in ministry to others. This insight is supported by David Moberg's research, reported in the chapter on "Community Programs and Services," to the effect that older persons are more involved in churches and synagogues than in all other types of social organization combined.

In the first place, the church, especially in its congregations, has unusual ability to bridge the gaps between generations — within its communal life, and within the families that make it up. Tensions develop between generations as a result of many factors, e.g. divergent points of view on childrearing, life-styles, moral values and political opinions, as well as practices within the church. These tensions, which often have immediately visible causes, are just as frequently made worse by misunderstanding, inadequate information, peer influence, and lack of patience. The church can help in many ways, for, after all, the church is one of the few institutions that bring together members of both sexes, various social classes, and all age groups.

If a congregation takes seriously its inherent ability to foster interchange within and among families and different groups of people, there are many creative things it can do. The gospel message that "God was in Christ reconciling the world to himself" is a powerful force to bring people together, resolve conflicts, and overcome enmity and guilt. To proclaim this good news is the church's primary task.

A congregation can develop programs that engage young, middle-aged and older persons in common fellowship and service activities and mutual discussions of matters of Christian concern.

A sensitive pastor or lay person can be an intermediary in crisis situations that arise between generations — an objective "third party" — as when such crucial questions are being faced as the care of the invalid father or mother, aunt or uncle.

Sometimes a congregation can serve as a substitute family for an elderly person who has no kin who live nearby or who care. The congregation is potentially a "healing community."

One way in which a congregation can help bridge the gaps that separate generations is to involve people of all ages in carrying important leadership responsibilities. Decisions about positions of leadership should be made on the basis of ability and interest rather than chronological age. The ministry of the church will benefit from the talents of persons of all ages sharing decisions and working together.

In the second place, the church has considerable ability to change societal values, both within its own life and within society. Earlier chapters of this book have described ageism, the negative image of aging and the older adult, which characterizes our general culture, the churches, and many of the elderly themselves. This pervasive attitude has caused discrimination against large numbers of older people, damaged their self-esteem, shriveled our concept of the totality of life, and reduced the contributions to society of a major segment of the population.

The church, however, *if it is willing* , can be an effective instrument in causing a profound turnabout from a negative to a positive image of aging. It has been given a dynamic faith, which enriches all of human experience and enables us to face every stage of life — and death — with eyes wide open. Dr. Martin Heinecken speaks of this in terms of the doctrine of vocation (calling). First, each person must pursue his or her calling from God, wherever he or she is at any time of life. And second, this legitimate "standing place" must not be taken away from the person, regardless of age or any other circumstance.

Furthermore, the church has been formed as a fellowship which in essence transcends all barriers and acknowledges the dignity of every human being, regardless of age, sex, color, class, and ethnic or national background. A congregation has the opportunity, through its worship and its educational resources, to give this faith and fellowship free course, to bring new perspectives to the total life span. It can foster a wholesome orientation to leisure as well as work, and toward sickness and health, disability and triumph over disability, retirement and bereavement, death and dying —all in the context of the cross and the resurrection of Jesus Christ. And since the church, both corporately and through its individual members, penetrates all areas of the larger community, it should see as a basic part of its business the attempt to change any of society's values which work against justice and human fulfillment and demean people, including those who are older.

In the third place, the church has special ability to serve the needs of older adults. Not the church by itself, to be sure. In this volume we have stressed that the church must be diligent and skillful in cooperating with the agencies of government, other churches, other community groups, and families. This is not a field in which unilateral, isolated action is to be recommended. Nevertheless, regardless of how many activities under various auspices may be going on in relation to the elderly, the church always has an essential contribution to make.

The church possesses a network of social service agencies and institutions, many of them devoting major attention to the elderly. The church is involved in community organizations and in housing projects for senior citizens. There are all kinds of programs in and among congregations — some highly sophisticated, using professional leadership and government funds; some very informal, depending upon volunteers and costing little. (See the chapter on "Community Programs and Services.")

The chief objective certainly is not to initiate a swarm of activities. It is rather to discover and develop what a congregation or a cluster of congregations, a district or a synod, an educational or social service agency or institution must *do* and *be* in its particular situation. And older adults themselves should be involved actively in the planning and implementation of whatever is projected.

An insidious temptation confronting the church — and every other institution or group, including the family — is to treat the elderly paternalistically. Surely such an approach violates the dignity of men and women, whether they are confined to nursing home beds or moving freely in our communities. Our sensitive care for the minority of the elderly who are physically and/or mentally ill should be matched by our equal respect and appreciation for the majority who are capable of continuing to make significant contributions to church and community. The church cannot hope to change society's destructive attitudes and discriminatory practices involving older adults unless these persons are enabled to participate as fully as every other group in the church's own life and ministry.

Summing Up

We began this chapter by stressing that the whole ministry of the church, though it has many manifestations, finds its unique basis in the Word and the sacraments. God's unconditional love is mediated through preaching and worship, counseling and pastoral care, evangelism and social ministry, through the ministry of individual clergy and laity, and through the ministry of the church as the community of faith.

Note: The National Interfaith Coalition on Aging (NICA) grew out of the "Spiritual Well Being" Section of the 1971 White House Conference on Aging. It is made up of some 25 Protestant, Roman Catholic, Eastern Orthodox, and Jewish Agencies, including the Division for Mission in North America of the Lutheran Church in America. In 1975 the coalition adopted the following definition of "Spiritual Well-Being:"

> Spiritual Well-Being is the affirmation of life in a relationship with God, self, community and environment that nurtures and celebrates wholeness.*

*National Interfaith Coalition on Aging, "Spiritual Well-Being."

9 Christian Perspectives on Aging

Christian Perspectives on Aging

Aging is ultimately a matter of life and death. To understand what it means to grow older, both for themselves and for others, Christians must be clear in their own minds about the theological basis for their thinking and living. Their appreciation of the later years — the opportunities and joys as well as the responsibilities, problems, and suffering — must become one with their conception of God, the church and the world.

No specific theology of aging can be developed in isolation from theology as a whole, just as there are no truly isolated doctrines of any kind. Creation, humanity, sin, redemption, sanctification, the church, grace, the new life, and the final destiny of humanity in the world — all these are parts of an integral whole. They must reflect the same basic understanding of God and of people's relationship to him and to one another.

So it is with aging. Our entire theology must be focused on this particular phase of life. It is essential also to stress the ethical implications that are inherent in the affirmations of faith which are made. An inclusive theological orientation is crucial to any consideration of the church's role in assuring older adults maximal freedom of choice in their living.

Just how much freedom of choice does any human being have? Is there a particular kind of Christian freedom? What presuppositions and limitations does it pose? Does "anything go"? Are there no positive guidelines, no prohibitions? And what is the church's role in this respect? Is it charged with peculiar responsibilities over against the community and the state? What resources does it offer that are uniquely its own?

The answers to these questions involve a total point of view — and we do not hesitate to say that the view here stated is avowedly confessional. It is based on a given revelation to which the Lutheran Church is striving to be faithful.

The Fundamental Affirmation: God's Unconditional Love

Without its basic affirmation of God's unconditional love for all creation (*agape*) the church would have no good news to proclaim afresh daily. So startling is this news that it can be given only in faith and in defiance of all evidence to the contrary in a broken world.

We have only one word for "love," and we tend to use it indiscriminately. We love everything from peanuts to baseball to a Bach concerto — from our friends, spouses and children, even to God Almighty. Surely the prize for defining love in our culture must go either to the beer ad, "If you like beer you'll love Schlitz!" or to the popular song, "I love little baby ducks, ol' pick up trucks, bourbon on the 'rucks,' and I love you too, baby!"

The Greeks were more discriminating. They had four words for love. The first, *agape,* is love that exists altogether for the sake of its object and not for the sake of any satisfaction gained from the beloved. This is unconditional, self-giving, suffering love that spends itself even for the unworthy, — even for the enemy. It is like the sun burning itself out to give the earth energy, receiving nothing for its light.

Such is the love of God who, as Martin Luther said, did not find the object of his love already there to supply a want in him, but rather created it out of nothing, that he might spend himself upon it in an ever-flowing fountain of love, a fiery abyss that never burns out.

If this is so, then not one of God's creatures is expendable. No human being is outside the sphere of his love. Not one is forgotten—no matter how loveless or burdensome or seemingly worthless, vicious or "good-for-nothing." All ages are equally precious to God. This is an incomparable gift that should make every heart sing and be joyful even in its darkest hour.

The Greeks' second word for love was *eros*, in myth the child of Plenty and Want. This is the love, therefore, that finds fulfillment in its object. This is the sense in which we most commonly speak of love — when we mean we "like" something. It gives us pleasure; it tickles our senses. But *eros* is by no means confined to the sexual; it also includes the satisfaction we experience from the pursuit of beauty, truth and goodness.

As finite beings, we need not only food, warmth and shelter, but also companionship. We need others, for there can be no solitary human being. There is only a person-in-relation, the individual-in-community. There are husbands, wives, children, friends, grandparents, grandchildren — an infinite variety, all unique and different, fulfilling the needs of others out of their plenty in a life-together-in-love!

But most of all, these finite and sinful persons are in need of God. Thus St. Augustine prayed: "Thou has made us, Lord, for thyself, and our hearts are restless within us until they rest in Thee."

Thirdly, the Greeks spoke of *filia* — the love of friendship, a selective love, one that chooses certain individuals above others for subjective reasons, whether because like is drawn to like or because opposites attract each other. How wonderful can be such a friendship between youth and old age!

Finally, the Greeks spoke of love in the sense of *libido,* the God-given sexual drive, which is not to be despised. Libido both seeks and gives satisfaction and enters subtly into all our relationships, since we are all sexual beings.

These four faces of love are interwoven in the lives of men and women who both give and receive. Our wants are fulfilled while at the same time we fulfill the wants of others. It is no trick to love ("like") the things and people that are lovable and give us satisfaction. It is much harder to love those who have little or nothing to give in return. It is hardest of all to love the enemy. Yet just such love is what we find embodied in Jesus, what he enjoins upon us. As members of the body of Christ, we are the channels through which this love flows from him to our neighbors. He is the vine; we are the branches (John 15).

Ethical Implications

We can readily see how this applies to the elderly. Not only are they beloved of God along with all other human beings, but they are also to be loved by humanity. They are to be loved for fulfilling the wants of others out of their plenty, their wisdom and their uniqueness. But they are not just to be used and then abandoned once their usefulness is over.

They are to be loved for their own sake as persons. They are to be loved and cared for even when they are no longer lovable, when they become a burden — even when they really do not "deserve" any care because somehow they have forfeited their just claims on other people.

This is particularly poignant where the aged are concerned. It is easy to care for a child in its lovable helplessness, because we are nurturing potential for the future. But when there no longer seems to be any potential, we feel only the burden. Then, love in the sense of *agape* must dominate our actions.

We can see how these four expressions of love are related to freedom of choice for the elderly. If we love them, we should provide resources for free choice. We can't just shunt them away — out of sight, out of mind — with other useless things. We must fully recognize their worth to society and dignity as human beings.

They must have full opportunity to make contributions according to their gifts. Their selection of friends and their sexuality must also be respected. If, for whatever reason, they are no longer capable of free choice, they must receive loving care as human beings and not just be rejected in some frightful way.

Nor should the aged allow themselves simply to vegetate or give way to self-indulgence. They should choose a way of life that enables them to make the most of what they still have left. The aged too are called to serve. But, on the other hand, they must not refuse to let themselves be served when that is necessary.

The Interrelation Between Justice and Love

The second basic affirmation of the church concerns the interrelation between justice and love. Justice is sometimes so defined as to be practically equivalent with love. But let us take it in its ordinary sense of fairness: giving each his due and treating equals as such while always taking differences into account. Justice is often depicted as blind, balancing the scales without respect of persons. Under justice, you get what you deserve and give your share. This concept requires just laws to safeguard essential rights, give everyone an equal chance, preserve order, punish offenders, and reward the law-abiding.

But love as *agape* breaks through the order of justice when that order does not deal out just deserts. Agape rather forgives offense and repays injury with kindness, hatred with love (Matt. 5:4ff). Yet this does not mean that justice has no proper place; in the realm of law love must first of all take the form of justice.

In a sinful world there must be just laws, justly enforced, to prevent the strong and ruthless from overpowering the weak and scrupulous. This is the "left hand" with which the God of love works his will in spite of human unwillingness to do right spontaneously. Institutions cannot be loving, but they can be just. People must have a framework of justice in order to relate freely with one another and go beyond justice to love. There is no virtue in eloquent talk about love if the speaker is not even just. There is nothing quite so devastating as offering high-handed charity to people who are only asking for their just rights.

In a just society every basic need of all the people, e.g. wages, housing, medical care and education, must be met in justice through the power of the law. This insistence falls within the realm of "civil righteousness." It stems from the assumption that all people are created in God's image, capable of a measure of justice and love within the limits of their finitude and sinfulness. God also recognizes this kind of "righteousness before men" as real "righteousness," although it has no merit to win us his favor.

Ethical Implications

The Christian interplay of justice and love is clearly relevant to freedom of choice in living for the elderly. Unless they have sufficient income and their basic needs are justly supplied, their freedom will be severely curtailed. In their earlier years individuals must be hard-working and provident and, so far as they can, must make provision for their old age. Their children, however, together with society, share the responsibility of providing for them in justice and then going beyond justice with love. For no matter how affluent the elderly may be, all the material comforts in the world will not make up for a lack of loving personal relationships.

The church's role is first of all to minister to all its people with the means of grace. Persons who enjoy forgiveness and new life will then be helped to develop their talents, cultivate civil virtues, and learn to deal justly in love with their fellow human beings. But in addition, the church must play the role of advocate in behalf of the elderly — as well as all others in need — to see that justice is done.

Human Freedom and Its Limitations

Human beings are not God,but they are created in his image (Gen. 1:26) as the crown of his creation, to be God's plenipotentiaries on earth and to steward it responsibly in his name. Just as rulers of old set up their likenesses in their territories to let everyone know who was sovereign there, so God has stamped us with his image.

We are created by the Word of God (John 1:3) as responsible persons, to respond to his Word out of our self-centered beings without coercion. We stand in a personal I-Thou relation to our Creator, answerable to him, subject to his will.

Ethical Implications

As creatures, we know that there are limits to our freedom. We are finite, with a beginning and an end in time. We are not the authors of our own lives, but rather are dependent on God's life-giving power for every breath we draw.

We are indeed free, we control our lives, but not absolutely. We are limited by both heredity and environment, and by other factors over which we have no control — above all, the constant threat of death. We have no absolute security in ourselves. Our limited freedom is always accompanied by a deep-seated dread, which, like a jammed organ pedal, keeps droning away beneath whatever music we make. We can escape from the anxiety of this insecurity only by coming to rest in the Power that created us, in the love of God that knows no bounds.

Human freedom is also limited by sinfulness. God calls upon his creatures to take their lives in trust and give them back to him in loving obedience.They are not free to make their own rules, but rather are subject to the law of God as it is written in their hearts (Romans 2:14), and revealed to them in the Mosaic law and, above all, in the life, words and works of Jesus the Christ.

This unique man Jesus was in every point tempted as we are, and yet he took his life from God and obeyed his will, becoming a perfect channel for his love. Confronted by Jesus we recognize ourselves as lifelong sinners, in need of forgiveness under God's judgment and dependent on his grace.

Baptism as the Basis for True Freedom

Baptism is of central importance to the Christian. It means unconditional acceptance by a gracious God and forms the basis for lifelong confidence. Before a person can do anything to win God's favor, God is there with his grace. Though no one can gain *security* in this life, we can all have *certainty* in God's steadfast love and everlasting forgiveness.

Baptism is thus the bulwark of the Christian's life. It frees from false religiosity, from all the "religious" things a person does to win God's favor. The redeemed child of God is freed for life in the world. The circle of self-centeredness is broken. Rather than doing good works to gain heaven, the Christian is free to serve the neighbor in love.

This liberation is important for older adults, lest they be tempted to devote their remaining years to "religious" practices in order to feather their nests in heaven.

Baptism also gives confidence in the face of death. There has recently been a widespread interest in life after death, as indicated by recent books by Elisabeth Kübler-Ross and Raymond A. Moody, Jr. The biblical promise is quite different from speculation about possible survival after death or supposed scientific proof of such survival.

The Bible takes death seriously as the end of life. It is *the* final mark of our finitude. We do not of ourselves, because of some inherent immortality, go on living when life leaves our bodies and they decay. We share the cycle of all living things — from the miracle of life's beginning through growth to maturity and then to decline, senescence, death and decay. In the biblical witness, moreover, death is regarded as the wages of sin (Romans 6:23). Because of our sinfulness we have no claim on eternal life; we can only receive it as a gift from a gracious God.

Ethical Implications

The Christian will, therefore, come to terms with death —but not just as part of the life cycle. That is resignation, not faith. Nor will the believer pin his hopes on all-too-flimsy evidences of survival. At best these yield a degree of probability that does not flow from personal trust in a living God. Besides, mere survival in another realm somewhat similar to the one we now inhabit is not at all what the Bible means by "the new heaven and the new earth" in which the "resurrected" will share.

Christians put their confidence in God and his promise. Conception means the gift of a brand-new, individual life from God, a miracle that is not just a hangover from a previous existence. The birth to newness of life in baptism is an equally miraculous gift, as a new person is born to live before God in righteousness forever. This means life as an individual-in-community, life together-in-love. It means a daily death of the old and rebirth of the new.

And when "death" finally comes — the end of the life cycle, the "wages" of sin, humanity's last bitter foe — then the Christian places his confidence in God and in the power of His resurrection. He who raised Jesus from the dead as "the first fruits of them that sleep" will also raise all persons for the final judgment. This resurrection is inseparable from the consummation of all things in a new heaven and a new earth beyond all human imagining.

It's not just more of the same as we have known life here in our finitude, insecurity, anxiety and sinfulness. Nor is it some kind of ethereal, bodiless existence that we ourselves can conjure up. What we can say with assurance — though we certainly do not know the "how" — is that it will be a life in fellowship with God and with one another as individuals-in-community. Those baptized by name will share in the table fellowship of which the Lord's Supper is a foretaste (Luke 22: 14-16; 1 Cor. 13:12).

Now what is the relevance of this assurance to freedom of choice for the elderly? It might, of course, be construed as mere solace, as "pie in the sky by and by." But, actually, it is a promise beside which all earthly glories dim. "For I consider that the sufferings of this present time are not worth comparing with the glory that is to be revealed to us."(Rom. 8:18)

Such a promise puts earthly life in proper perspective. It forms the basis of true Christian freedom, which enables us to be *in* the world but not *of* it. And, because of this final consummation, undreamed-of things can happen also in this present life.

The Christian Serving in His "Standing Place"

Finally, service to others where they are is the hallmark of an evangelical orientation. Christians should serve in all the places to which destiny and freedom lead them. In love, they should meet the needs of the moment as best they can, trusting in God's forgiveness in the midst of the inevitable conflict of duties. Only thus can the work of a sinful world be accomplished.

The expression "standing place" is a literal translation of the German *Stand-ort*. In Luther's day those Christians who wanted to make sure of reaching "perfection" left their ordinary occupations and fled into monasteries and convents, where they thought they could live a holier life and gain God's favor. But Luther rediscovered the gospel that a person is justified fully before God by grace alone, through faith. God in Christ has done everything necessary for his or her salvation. Thus the Christian is freed from any need to perform "religious" works, freed to serve the neighbor *in* the world.

Each person has multiple responsibilities that depend on both a given destiny and a free choice. At one and the same time, a person may be a son or daughter, a brother or sister, a husband or wife, a breadwinner and a neighbor. He or she may be a farmer, a banker, a politician, a doctor or a soldier —involved in a sinful world and yet charged with clear responsibilities that conflict with one another. As Christians we cannot opt out of this kind of sinful involvement. There is no neat set of rules for us to follow to keep our record clean. There is no way to do God's will in a sinful world except as we meet the demands of our "standing place." If a policeman, for example, must kill in order to promote justice and keep order, he is doing what his "standing place" calls for, and he must trust God to forgive the taking of a life.

Ethical Implications

Old age as one's inevitable destiny usually begins at a time when a measure of freedom is still available. Just what the older person should do with her or his life cannot be blueprinted in advance. It depends on the "standing place," together with any number of factors — sex, marital status, income, locality, health, strength, talents, obligations. What an awesome responsibility, for example, if you happen to be a grandfather! Equally awesome responsibilities may rest upon the shoulders of one who has never married! Who can prescribe for another?

One person may still have obligations to relatives which should be met. One may still have strengths and talents to serve church and community in a variety of ways. Another may be dependent on others, yet within that limitation is able to serve in love. Still another may be capable of doing little, but will need to learn to accept service gratefully. It all depends on their "standing place."

So it is clear that older adults, like everyone else, will have to make responsible decisions that are appropriate in every time and place. And the church and society should work to achieve the fullest freedom possible for them to realize their God-given destiny.

Appendices

APPENDIX I.
A Social Statement of the Lutheran Church in America

Aging and the Older Adult

Adopted by the Ninth Biennial Convention, Chicago,Illinois
July 12 - 19, 1978

Life is a gift of God, and aging is a natural part of living.

More positive attitudes toward the aging process and toward older adults are a profound need today. Men and women 65 years of age and over now constitute one-tenth of the population of Canada and the United States. A vast number of older adults are able and willing to function effectively throughout their lives, serving their congregations and communities, and adding their strength in the struggle to achieve justice for all.

Aging: Prejudice and Injustice

Too often negative attitudes within our society place unnecessary restrictions upon the freedom of the elderly. Frequently the media portray older adults as tottering, forgetful, slow-witted and helpless. Prejudicial attitudes result in injustice toward a large number of older people and deprive society of their talent, experience and wisdom. They are forced too readily into retirement, often eased out of responsible leadership positions in the church and community, too frequently "protected" from making life-affecting decisions, and in some instances made the objects of service activities that other well-meaning persons plan and administer.

People in our work-oriented society tend to view personal dignity largely in terms of occupational performance. As a consequence, loss of occupation or retirement frequently results in the loss of one's sense of dignity. While acknowledging the many problems that arise from unemployment or retirement, this church nevertheless affirms that human dignity has a far deeper foundation than work or status.

Theological Affirmations

God's love for all persons is creative and unconditional. Human beings have dignity not because they have achieved success or the esteem of the world, but because they are made in the image of God. They are given the capacity to relate to God in responsible freedom.

However, in sinful rebellion against God, old and young alike frequently act unreasonably and irresponsibly toward each other. As one consequence , older adults often become the undeserving victims of prejudice and discrimination in the callous abuse of their dignity and rights.

The Christian faith looks at all of human existence, its joy and its suffering, in the light of the cross and resurrection of Jesus Christ. It takes seriously both life and death, declares God's promise that the sting of death is overcome by the resurrection of Christ, and testifies that forgiveness and new life are granted to the faithful in daily and eternal fellowship with God. This Christian view of the aging process gives reason for joy and hope at every stage.

By God's action in Holy Baptism, we are commissioned to "lead a life worthy of the calling to which we have been called" (Ephesians 4:1). This calling — vocation — empowers us to live for others by faithfully serving our neighbors in love and justice. We receive varieties of gifts, which the Holy Spirit enables us to use in building up the body of Christ in witness and service in the world.

Older members of the church have skills, wisdom, and experience to share in exercising the universal priesthood of the baptized. The Spirit helps us to discern the special gifts and needs of the elderly, along with the related opportunities and obligations of Christians in society.

A chief way in which God deals with the human condition in society is to provide all people with civil authority in order to advance the well-being and to secure equal opportunity for the full development of all citizens. Persons are given reason and conscience to help them determine and seek what is just. For older adults, government shares in this responsibility with the elderly themselves, the family, the church, religious and voluntary organizations, business firms, labor unions and other social institutions and structures.

Agenda for Action

This church affirms the God-given dignity of human beings of all ages. It emphasizes their right and responsibility to make important decisions and to choose ways in which to participate in the family, the church, and the community. It sees them as individual persons, each different from others in background, life experiences, talents, interests, and present circumstances.

This church understands that many older adults continue to learn, to be open to new ideas, to enjoy a wide variety of interpersonal relationships, including their sexuality, and to engage in constructive activity. But this church also acknowledges that it should respond with sensitivity and skill to the special needs of those who are ill, handicapped, lonely and discouraged.

The church sets forth the following agenda for purposeful action:

Families

Human beings, whatever their age, are to be viewed not as individuals in isolation from one another, but as persons in community. One basic expression of community is the family. In a time when "family" is frequently viewed in two-generational terms — father, mother, and their children — older members often find themselves set apart from the extended family group, treated as outsiders or invited guests, and deprived of the warm acceptance they cherish.

Whether or not there are severe problems in such areas as income and health, older adults may be even more distressed by a sense of alienation from life, especially if it involves unsatisfactory relationships with the younger generations. This tendency to alienation is often associated with such factors as family mobility, differing opinions regarding the rearing of children, and the smaller size of living accommodations. Tensions may be increased by the effect the disabilities of older persons may have on younger relatives, by difficult decisions that families must make, by lack of effective communication, or by feelings of inadequacy and guilt on both sides.

It is essential to the well-being of all that older men and women be given honor and loving respect, and that in this spirit they be acknowledged as full members of their own families, even if geographically separated, living in an institutional setting, or mentally or physically incapacitated. Every effort must be made to foster wholesome exchange of ideas, sensitive understanding, and mutual communication and helpfulness among generations.

Congregations

This church should seek older women and men, as it seeks other persons, both as members and as full participants in all dimensions of parish life. Older members are called to share in worship, learning, witness, service and support according to their personal abilities and interests. The congregation is potentially well qualified to engage persons of all ages in activities and relationships which encourage understanding and fellowship across generational lines.

The congregation as a community of faith has unrivaled opportunity to assist people, including older men and women, when they experience changes in living arrangements, loss of social esteem or physical capacity, and illness. This is especially true when Christians face the death of spouse, other family members or friends, and ultimately their own death. Through its ministry of Word and sacrament, its educational ministry, its supportive fellowship and spiritual nurture, the congregation can help persons cope with such experiences.

The congregation, recognizing that both the positive and negative attitudes of society are found among kinfolk, should strengthen and provide resources to the family as it relates to its older members. It should help the family to cultivate love and respect and a sense of mutual responsibility across the generations, and to be a constructive healing force in all its relationships. The congregation should show equal concern for older persons who are isolated or alienated. Such men and women often have greater needs than do those with a supportive family. It is necessary, therefore, that they be provided with or alerted to alternate supportive relationships, including the congregation's own role as an "extended family."

In seeking to help older adults with their social and material needs, the congregation should concentrate on encouraging the community to provide essential services. Within this larger setting it can either offer or join with others in offering supportive programs. These may include visiting, telephone reassurance, home health care, chore service, transportation assistance, congregate meals or meals delivered in homes, financial help to meet special needs, senior center activities, and guidance to its people in using community resources. The congregation should make every effort to assure that its buildings afford easy access and free mobility for all persons, and, wherever advisable and feasible, make those buildings available for community programs.

In whatever is done, older women and men ought to carry an important share of responsibility for planning and operating programs. Every effort should be made to respect their dignity, and to remember that bedridden as well as healthy persons wish to be accepted members of society and are often capable of enriching or rendering service to others.

Synods

This church should advance the well-being of older adults by:

1) assisting congregations in their ministries with the elderly, using the skills and leadership of educational and social service agencies and institutions wherever feasible;
2) maintaining supportive relationships with church-related agencies and institutions that are engaged in this field;
3) advocating with provincial/state and local governments concerning the rights and needs of older persons;
4) advocating with provincial/state and local governments on behalf of church-related agencies and institutions to encourage the establishment of adequate levels of reimbursement for covered services provided by said agencies and institutions to eligible recipients;
5) availing themselves of and referring congregations and individuals to the resources of governmental and nongovernmental organizations working with the elderly, and cooperating with such organizations in mutual endeavor;
6) conducting training workshops for persons involved in ministry with older persons; and
7) providing guidance and leadership for programs, workshops and seminars on the aging process, avoidable factors that accelerate aging, attitudes toward older adults, and pre-retirement planning.

Each synod should assign responsibility for these tasks to a specific program unit, new or existing, and include older men and women in its planning and leadership.

Social Service Agencies and Institutions

This church should affirm the ministries of social service agencies and institutions related to it which work with older adults. As it requires these agencies and institutions to meet the highest standards of health, safety, and service, this church encourages them in their efforts:

1) to assist synods to support area congregations in carrying out their ministries with older adults;
2) to design programs which assist older adults to continue to be integral members of society;
3) to provide supportive services—physical, emotional, social, spiritual— which enable older men and women to maintain independent living arrangements as long as feasible;
4) to provide services which protect older adults from abuse and exploitation, whether physical, emotional or economic;
5) to provide supportive services which enable ill or disabled older persons to receive sensitive care in the homes of their families, or in other residential settings;
6) to improve the physical, mental, emotional, and spiritual well-being of the elderly in institutionalized/specialized care;
7) to develop institutional living arrangements and programs that affirm the sexuality of older adults;
8) to place buildings in geographical locations and make structural provisions that assure maximum access to all persons;
9) to serve and employ low income older persons whenever possible;
10) to advocate public policies and regulations that assure that church-related and other voluntary agencies or institutions are not made the objects of discrimination when they endeavor to obtain public funds in return for services they provide to the community; and
11) to use academic resources in gerontology and other disciplines to help with these tasks.

Higher Education

This church encourages the colleges, universities, and campus ministries related to it in their efforts:

1) to motivate and equip faculty and students to see education as a lifelong process;
2) to extend opportunities for middle-aged and older persons to participate in formal educational programs;
3) to sponsor courses, seminars, and intergenerational activities

regarding older adults and aging which involve faculty, students, alumni and the general public;

4) to enable the participation of faculty and students in church and community programs working with the elderly;
5) to assist in training personnel for agencies and institutions which render direct services to older persons; and
6) to use academic resources in gerontology to help with these tasks.

Theological Seminaries

This church encourages theological seminaries in their efforts:

1) to equip pastors and other professional leaders with information and skills with regard to aging;
2) to extend opportunities for middle-aged and older persons to participate in formal education programs;
3) to sponsor seminars, workshops, and related activities which foster constructive attitudes among faculty, students, alumni and the general public toward older persons and aging;
4) to enable the participation of faculty and students in church and community programs working with the elderly; and
5) to use academic resources in gerontology and other disciplines to help with these tasks.

Retirement Policies of this Church

This church, in dealing with older adults, should be concerned to practice the best stewardship of human resources in its own employment and retirement policies.

Public Policy

This church, both through the daily lives of its members and through its corporate actions, seeks changes in society toward a more positive image of aging and greater justice for the elderly. It views this endeavor as part of the promotion of justice for all people, and recognizes that many older adults are ready to serve as leaders and participants.

Therefore, this church declares itself in support of the following public policy goals:

1) Adequate income for all older persons,derived from an effective

combination of personal resources, pension plans, continuing income from work, and government social insurance and income support programs.

2) Food policies and programs (including nutrition education) which benefit the elderly, especially the poor, the homebound, and the isolated.
3) Action and funding to help secure adequate housing of sufficient variety to offer alternatives in living arrangements for older adults, including those without the ability to pay the full costs.
4) A comprehensive health care program ensuring equity in access to services and facilities and freedom from fear of catastrophic medical costs; a program funded through fair and equitable means, with risks spread over the entire population.*
5) Responsible government fiscal policies which recognize the impact which inflation has upon the elderly, and which seek to contain inflation by providing more efficient delivery of human services and by moderating federal spending for those programs not directly related to human services.
6) Elimination or avoidance of injurious age discrimination in employment and retirement practices in government, business, and industry.
7) Exploration of ways by which business and other types of organizations may use the experience and counsel of older adults, and may develop more effective programs that prepare workers for retirement.
8) Structural provisions in public buildings that assure easy access and free mobility for infirm and handicapped persons, large numbers of whom are elderly.
9) Supportive services which enable persons to maintain independent living in their communities as long as feasible; and skilled care in institutions, including hospices, for all who require it, provided in ways that respect the dignity of the individual in the right of self-determination with regard to his or her own person so that family and community ties may be continued.
10) Legal assistance and law enforcement which protect the rights and provide for the safety of older men and women.

* Canada has such a program.

11) Educational programs, under private and public auspices, available to people of all ages.
12) Cultivation of constructive attitudes toward aging and the older adult in areas such as the communications media and educational institutions.
13) Encouragement of cultural institutions and programs to recognize older adults as part of their constituency — as volunteers, paid professionals, and audiences.

Conclusion

All persons have worth and dignity because they are created in God's image. This church calls upon its members and all elements of its corporate life to embody this truth in all their relationships, especially — in the context of this statement — those affecting older adults.

APPENDIX II.
Resources

A. Bibliography

Books for General Reading

Bortz, Edward L. *Creative Aging*. New York: The Macmillan Company, 1963.

An excellent overview of the problems and potentials of older adults, dealt with by a well-known geriatrist in such a way as to stress the meaning of the title, "Creative Aging."

Comfort, Alex. *A Good Age*. New York: Crown Publishers, 1976.

A highly readable book which attacks ageism and calls for positive attitudes toward the later years.

Curtin, Sharon R. *Nobody Ever Died of Old Age*. Boston: Little, Brown and Company, 1973.

A personal survey of the variety of life-styles adopted by old people in America, in which the author calls upon the elderly to organize and take control of their own lives. This touching, poignant, unsentimental, sometimes humorous and always potent piece of writing should, for a long time to come, serve America's aged as a manifesto for action.

Maclay, Elise. *Green Winter: Celebrations of Old Age*. New York: Reader's Digest Press, distributed by Thomas Y. Crowell Company, 1977.

Nouwen, Henri. *Aging*. New York: Doubleday and Company, 1974.

A highly readable little book in which photographs by Walter Gaffney enhance the author's perceptive writing about aging.

Scott-Maxwell, Florida. *The Measure of My Days*. New York: Alfred A. Knopf, 1973.

A moving book in which eighty-two-year-old Mrs. Scott-Maxwell shares her insights about her full life from the perspective of the later years.

Smith, Bert Kruger. *Aging in America.* Boston: Beacon Press, 1973.

* An evocative guide to the problems of the aging, in the context of a positive attitude.

Tournier, Paul. *Learn to Grow Old.* New York: Harper and Row, 1971.

An excellent theological-psychological interpretation by the Swiss psychiatrist and lay theologian.

Basic Books for Study

Beauvoir, Simone de. *The Coming of Age*, New York: G.P. Putnam's Sons, 1972. Now available in paperback.

The classic in the field, Mme. de Beauvoir's engrossing work expresses what it means and how it feels to become old, to join that underprivileged and disadvantaged minority toward which society must change its attitudes.

Butler, Robert N. *Why Survive? Being Old in America.* New York: Harper and Row, 1975.

A thoroughly-documented book that "balances the grim reality of what it is like to be old in America against the pieties that deny that reality." Very readable.

Environics Research Group. *The Seventh Age.* Policy Planning Division, Central Mortgage and Housing Corporation, Ottawa, Canada.

A bibliography of Canadian Sources in gerontology and geriatrics, 1964-1972.

National Council on the Aging, Inc. *The Myth and Reality of Aging in America,* 1975. Obtain from NCOA, 1828 L Street, N.W., Washington, DC 20036.

Report of a major study made for NCOA by Louis Harris and Associates, Inc., of the attitudes and perceptions of the American public with regard to aging.

1.* Older Adults in Society

Atchley, Robert C. *The Social Forces in Later Life: An Introduction to Social Gerontology*. Belmont, CA: Wadsworth Publishing Company, 1972.

**Numbers of bibliography sections correspond with chapter numbers.*

Field, Minna. *The Aged, The Family, and the Community.* New York: Columbia University Press, 1972.

Neugarten, Bernice L. (ed.). *Middle Age and Aging.* Chicago: University of Chicago Press, 1968.

Sarton, May. *As We Are Now.* New York: W.W. Norton, 1973.

Silverstone, Barbara, and Hyman, Helen K. *You and Your Aging Parent: The Modern Family's Guide to Emotional, Physical & Financial Problems.* New York: Pantheon Press, 1976.

Spicker, Stuart F., Woodward, Kathleen M., and Van Tassel, David D. (eds.) *Aging and the Elderly: Humanistic Perspectives in Gerontology.* Atlantic Highlands, NJ: Humanities Press, Text Edition, 1978.

2. Psychology of Aging

Birren, James E. *The Psychology of Aging.* Englewood Cliffs, NJ: Prentice-Hall, 1964.

Caine, Lynn. *Widow.* New York: Bantam Books, 1975. Paperback.

Eisdorfer, Carl and Lawton, M. Powell (eds.). *The Psychology of Adult Development and Aging.* Washington DC: American Psychological Association, 1973. Paperback.

Kreis, Bernadine and Pattie, Alice. *Up From Grief: Patterns of Recovery.* New York: Seabury Press, 1969.

Kübler-Ross, Elisabeth. *On Death and Dying.* New York: The Macmillan Company, 1969.

Lynch, James J. *The Broken Heart: The Medical Consequences of Loneliness.* Basic Books, 1977.

Saxon, Sue V. and Etten, Mary Jean. *Physical Change and Aging: A Guide for the Helping Professions.* New York: The Tiresias Press, 1978. Paperback.

Weibe, Katie E. *Alone.* Wheaton, IL: Tyndale House Publishers, Inc., 1976.

Westberg, Granger E. *Good Grief.* Philadelphia: Fortress Press, 1962.

3. Living the Older Years in Health

Butler, Robert N. and Lewis, Myrna I. *Sex After Sixty.* New York:

Harper & Row, 1976. Available in paperback from Harper & Row under title of *Love and Sex After Sixty*.

Eisdorfer, Carl. *The Role of the Psychiatrists*. Successful Aging, A Conference Report. Durham, NC: Center for the Study of Aging and Human Development, Duke University, 1974.

Exercises While You Watch TV. Sickroom Services, Inc., 2534 S. Kinnickinnic Avenue, Milwaukee, WI 53207, 1976.

Higdon, Hal. *Fitness After Forty*. CA: World Publications, 1977.

Hrachovec, Joseph P. *Keeping Young and Living Longer*. Los Angeles: Sherbourne Press, 1973.

Mendelsohn, Mary Adelaide. *Tender Loving Greed*. New York: Alfred A. Knopf, 1974.

Schneider, Karl A. *Alcoholism and Addiction: A Study Program for Adults and Youth*. Philadelphia: Fortress Press, 1976.

The Fitness Challenge... An Exercise Program for Older Americans. HEW Publication No. (OHD) 75-10802, reprinted July, 1975. Administration on Aging, Washington, DC 20201.

Woodruff, Diana S. *Can You Live to be 100?* New York: New American Library, paperback, 1979. Chatham Square, hardback, 1977.

4. Living Arrangements

American Nursing Home Association. *Thinking About a Nursing Home?* Washington, DC: American Nursing Home Association, 1973.

Atchley, Robert C. and Miller, Sheila J. "Housing of the Rural Aged." In Robert C. Atchley (ed.), *Environments and the Rural Aged*. Washington, DC: The Gerontological Society, 1975.

Beyer, Glenn H. *Housing and Society*. New York: The Macmillan Company, 1963.

Council on Better Business Bureaus. *Tips on Buying a Mobile Home*. Washington, DC, 1978.

Ford, Norman D. *Where to Retire on a Small Income*. New York: Harian Publications, 1977.

Jacobs, Jane. *The Death and Life of Great American Cities*. New York: Random House, 1961.

Keith, Nathaniel S. *Politics and the Housing Crisis Since 1930*.

New York: Universe Books, 1973.

National Council on the Aging. *Guide for Selection of Retirement Housing.* Washington, DC, 1976.

U.S. Senate Special Committee on Aging. "Older Americans in Rural Areas." Report of a series of hearings in 1970 and 1971. U.S.Government Printing Office, 1971.

———*The Multiple Hazards of Age and Race: The Situation of Aged Blacks in the United States.* A working paper, preliminary survey prepared by Dr. Inabel B. Lindsay. Washington, D.C.: U.S. Government Printing Office, September 1971.

———Subcommittee on Housing for the Elderly. *Homeowner Aspects of the Economics of Aging.* U.S. Government Printing Office, 1969.

Willner, Robert F. *Criteria for Long-term Care Placement: Referral Guidelines for the Clergy.* St. Louis: The Catholic Hospital Association, 1979.

5. Education

AIM Guidebooks (On retirement preparation), Action for Independent Maturity, P.O. Box 2240, Long Beach, CA, 90801. Single copies free on request. Multiple copies (minimum of five per order) available for 20¢ each. Titles: *Financial Security, Dynamic Fitness, Home and Personal Safety, Legal Readiness, Housing Choices, The Time in Your Life, Your Vital Papers, Communication in Marriage, Alcohol in the Middle Years, Single Living, Planning Your Retirement, Estate Planning,* and *Midlife Roles and Goals.*

De Crow, Roger. *New Learning for Older Americans: An Overview of National Effort.* Washington, DC: Adult Education Association, 1975.

Hunter, Woodrow W. *Preparation for Retirement.* The Institute of Gerontology, University of Michigan—Wayne State University, Ann Arbor, MI, 1976.

Korim, A.S. *Older Americans and Community Colleges: A Guide for Program Implementation.* Washington, DC: American Association of Community and Junior Colleges, 1974.

National Council on the Aging, Senior Centers Humanities Program, 1828 L Street, N.W., Suite 504, Washington, DC 20035. An innovative effort to involve older Americans in

Literature, Drama, History, Philosophy, Ethics and the Arts. Write to NCOA at above address.

Otte, Elmer. *Rehearse Before You Retire.* Appleton, WI: Retirement Research, 1970.

———*Welcome Retirement.* St. Louis: Concordia Publishing House, 1974.

Wolf, Betty and Umhau. *Ten to Get Ready: Preparing for Retirement.* Philadelphia: Fortress Press, 1977

6. Community Programs and Services

Hall, Gertrude H. and Mathiasen, Geneva (eds.) *Guide to Development of Protective Services for Older People.* Springfield, IL: Charles C. Thomas, 1973.

Lawton, M. Powell and Byerts, T. (eds.). *Community Planning for the Elderly.* Washington, DC: The Gerontological Society, 1973.

"Quality In Home Supportive Services." Monographs issued by National Voluntary Organizations for Independent Living for the Aging (NVOILA). Washington, DC: National Council on the Aging, 1828 L Street, N.W., Suite 504, 1978.

Taietz, Philip. "Community Facilities and Social Services." In Robert C. Atchley (ed.), *Environment and the Rural Aged.* Washington, DC: The Gerontological Society, 1975.

Terris, Bruce J. *Legal Services for the Elderly.* Washington, DC: National Council on the Aging, 1972.

U.S. Senate Special Committee on Aging. *Home Health Services in the United States: A Working Paper on Current Status.* Washington, DC: U.S. Government Printing Office, 1973.

———*Older Americans and Transportation. A Crisis in Mobility.* Washington, DC: U.S. Government Printing Office, 1970.

———Subcommittee on Federal, State and Community Services. *The Rise and Threatened Fall of Service Programs for the Elderly.* Washington, DC: U.S. Government Printing Office, 1973.

7. Finances in the Later Years

Ford, Norman D. *How to Increase Your Retirement and Other*

Income. New York: Harian Publications, 1968.

Health and Welfare Canada. *Basic Facts on Social Security Programs.* A pocket reference guide, July 1977. Copies available from Director, Information Productions Division, Welfare Information Systems Branch, Room 1232, Brooke Claxton Building, Tunney's Pasture, Ottawa, Canada K1A 0K9.

Hoffman, Ray. *Extra Dollars: Easy Money-Making for Retired People.* New York: Stein and Day, 1977.

Jaffee, A.J. *The Middle Years. Neither Too Young Nor Too Old.* Washington, DC : National Council on the Aging, 1971.

Kreps, Juanita M. *Lifetime Allocation of Work and Income. Essays in the Economics of Aging.* Durham, NC: Duke University Press, 1971.

Porter, Sylvia. *Sylvia Porter's Money Book.* New York: Avon Books, 1976. Paperback.

Research Institute of America, 589 Fifth Avenue, New York, NY 10017. *What You Should Know About Your Social Security Now.*

Three Budgets for a Retired Couple. U.S. Bureau of Labor Statistics, Department of Labor, Washington, DC 20212, 1977.

8 and 9. The Church and Aging

Brown, J. Paul. *Counseling with Senior Citizens.* Philadelphia: Fortress Press, 1971.

Clements, William M. *Care and Counseling of the Aging.* Philadelphia: Fortress Press, 1979.

Clingan, Donald F. *Aging Persons in the Community of Faith.* St. Louis: The Christian Board of Publication, 1975.

Cook, Thomas C., Jr. *The Religious Sector Explores its Mission in Aging.* Report of a major study of religious programs on aging made by the National Interfaith Coalition on Aging, Inc. Write NICA at 298 S. Hull Street (Box 1924), Athens, GA 30601.

Cook, Thomas C. and Thorsen, James (eds.). *Spiritual Well-Being of the Elderly.* Springfield, IL: Charles C. Thomas, 1980.

Ebinger, Mary R. *I Was Sick and You Visited Me.* Women's Division, Board of Global Ministries, the United Methodist

Church. Order from Service Center, Board of Global Ministries, 7820 Reading Road, Cincinnati, OH 45237 (35 cents).

Gray, Robert M. and Moberg, David O. *The Church and the Older Person.* Grand Rapids, MI: Eerdmans, 1962 (revised, 1977). Available in paperback.

Heinecken, Martin J. and Hellerich, Ralph R. *The Church's Ministry with Older Adults: A Theological Basis.* New York: Division for Mission in North America, Lutheran Church in America, 231 Madison Avenue, 1976 ($1.50).

McClellan, Robert W. *Claiming a Frontier: Ministry and Older People.* Los Angeles: USC Press, 1977. Publication Office, Andrus Gerontology Center, University Park, Los Angeles, CA 90007.

"Project Compassion." A Visitor's Kit and a Supervisor's Kit. The Board of Social Ministry and World Relief, Lutheran Church-Missouri Synod, 500 North Broadway, St. Louis, MO 63102.

Walker, H. Thomas. *Because We Care: How to Organize a Lay Ministry with Shut-ins.* Order from the Service Center, Board of Global Ministries, 7820 Reading Road, Cincinnati, OH 45237 ($1.50).

B. 16 mm Films

Portrait of Grandpa Doc

28 minutes, color, rental fee: $45.00

The story of a boy's relationship with his grandfather, a retired physician. The boy is an artist. As he is preparing for an exhibit we see flashbacks to his childhood summers spent with his grandfather at his home at the shore. "Grandpa Doc" encouraged the young man's artistic pursuits and contributed to his growth in other areas as well. The exhibit turns out to be a loving tribute to Grandpa Doc, now dead.

Phoenix Films
470 Park Avenue South
New York, NY 10016

At 99, A Portrait Of Louise Tandy Murch

24 minutes, color, rental fee: $18.00

The film opens at Mrs. Murch's 99th birthday party, where she is surrounded by her family and friends. Later, we see her in a more normal daily life, living alone in the house she has occupied for 61 years. She discovered (and practices each day) yoga at age 91. A very warm portrait.

Film Rental Center of Syracuse University
1455 East Colvin Street
Syracuse, NY 13210

Don't Stop The Music

18 minutes, color, free rental

People do not suddenly change life-styles when they reach 60 or 65. In this film older adults speak for themselves, dispelling myths as they show their capacity for enjoyment, productivity, and an active life. Problems are depicted too. The film examines ways communities can help.

Modern Talking Picture Service
232 New Hyde Park Road
New Hyde Park, NY 11050

A Walk Up The Hill

30 minutes, color, rental fee: $25.00

At age 77, Dr. Wakefield has plans for a new career. An associate will take over his medical practice and he will open a dairy farm. In the midst of the retirement festivities, he suffers a stroke. He tells his associate not to let him linger. A second, more severe stroke leaves him totally paralyzed and speechless. Whenever a difficult decision had to be made, Dr. Wakefield would "walk up the hill" to be alone with God. Now his associate, Dr. Hughes, "walks up the hill" to decide whether to prolong Wakefield's life by artificial means or let him die. Longer life spans and medical advances have made euthanasia a concern of modern society. This film examines this concern from a Christian perspective.

Fortress Church Supply Stores Films Department

36 Wabash Avenue
Chicago, IL 60603

122 West Franklin Avenue
Minneapolis, MN 55404

2900 Queen Lane
Philadelphia, PA 19129

Hello in There

21 minutes, color, rental fee: $23.00

This film dramatizes the story of Mary, a widow in a boringly sterile retirement home, who creates imaginative ways to escape the mindless monotony of the home. She writes letters to herself just to receive some mail, and she shoplifts just to gain attention. Mary is a "survivor." She has lived through the pain of loss after the death of her husband of 48 years. Her children have grown up and moved away, and her friends have gone, one by one. However, Mary finds some solace from her loneliness in a once-a-week visit to her husband's grave, and in her bus trip to a downtown shopping area, which, as she laments, is changing too.

TeleKETICS
1229 S. Santee Street
Los Angeles, CA 90015

Journey's End

28 minutes, color, rental fee: $25.00

The film stresses the importance of making essential preparations for death — long-range planning, preparation of wills, specifying funeral arrangements.

The Ethel Percy Andrus Gerontology Center
University of Southern California
University Park
Los Angeles, CA 90007

NRTA/AARP
Public Relations
1909 K Street, N.W.
Washington, DC 20049

Tomorrow Comes Early

25 minutes, color, rental fee: $20.00

Paul Butram, a middle-aged college professor, hears his doctor tell him to slow down. But Paul, like so many of us, doesn't want to believe that he is aging. His trauma and personal search for self-affirmation is captured in surrealistic sequences, multiple flashbacks, and other dramatic cinematic effects as we discover with Paul that age and maturity is a gift from God — not a penalty.

Fortress Church Supply Stores Films Department

36 Wabash Avenue
Chicago, IL 60603

122 West Franklin Avenue
Minneapolis, MN 55404

2900 Queen Lane
Philadelphia, PA 19129

Old Fashioned Woman

50 minutes, color, rental fee: $30.00

A mellow and admiring portrait of an 86-year old Yankee, who not only airs her views on birth control and abortion, but considers the approach of her own death with a gentle dignity. The filmmaker/granddaughter inserts herself into her own film as interrogator and fond grandchild.

Film Rental Center of Syracuse University
1455 East Colvin Street
Syracuse, NY 13210

Peege

28 minutes, color, rental fee: $40.00

A family visits the aged grandmother in a nursing home. The visit is awkward, but when the family leaves, the oldest grandson stays behind. His efforts to bring a genuine response succeed, so that he manages to give her a feeling of self-worth because she knows someone cares. An excellent discussion-starter.

Phoenix Films
470 Park Avenue South
New York, NY 10016

Sykes

13 minutes, color, rental fee: $18.00

Sykes Williams. Gutsy. Irish. Blind. A storyteller. Sykes and his wife live in a run-down Chicago neighborhood. He plays piano two nights a week in a bar to supplement his pension. His amiable banter is spiced with complaints about lack of respect for the elderly... inadequate social security. This is more than a story about growing old. This is a story of a proud man, living an active, meaningful life.

Film Rental Center of Syracuse University
1455 East Colvin Street
Syracuse, NY 13210

Minnie Remembers

5 minutes, color, rental fee: $12.50

A poem made into a movie, this film makes a simple statement about old age and loneliness in a beautiful and effective manner.

Mass Media Ministries
2116 N. Charles Street
Baltimore, MD 21218

The Stringbean

17 minutes, black & white, rental fee: $15.00

A bean seed is cultivated into a stalk by a lonely old woman. As it grows, it lessens the drabness of her surroundings. She transplants the stalk to the flower bed of a neighboring park. A caretaker uproots the stalk but the old woman recovers one of the pods from the trash heap — determined to keep the loveliness of new life nearby. Beautifully understated, this film can be understood at many levels.

Mass Media Ministries
2116 N. Charles Street
Baltimore, MD 21218

Fortress Church Supply Stores
Films Department
2900 Queen Lane
Philadelphia, PA 19129

The Joy of Communication

18 minutes, color, rental fee: $22.50

The film depicts communication among people of all ages showing the reciprocal joy of sharing values and experiences — between young and old, parents and children, teacher and student, including the handicapped. The joy of communicating with nature is also portrayed, as well as the joy in an old person's face with the realization that he or she is needed. For adult groups, especially suitable for encouraging senior citizens to remain active forces in their communities.

Concordia Publishing House
Audiovisual Media
3558 South Jefferson Avenue
St. Louis, MO 63118

Trigger Films On Aging

1 - 4 minutes each, color

Brief, evocative, color films designed to trigger discussion. Developed in 1971 for state and national White House Conferences on Aging, they succinctly illustrate some of the problems of growing old in North America. They stop short of the information endings, leaving the audience to supply the conclusion — to discuss the problems. The Trigger films won major awards at the U.S. Industrial Film Festival and the Venice Film Festival.

University of Michigan Television Center
408 South Fourth Street
Ann Arbor, MI 48109

The Shopping Bag Lady
21 minutes, color, rental fee: $16.50

Emily and her friends are rather typical 14 year old girls, busy with school, bubbling with energy, and oblivious to other people's problems and needs; elderly people seem only to be nuisances. One day in New York they come across an old woman who is destitute and alone. The girls take no pains to hide their disdain for the old woman. Sometime later the old lady takes one of the girl's brothers for a walk. Emily's friend calls a policeman and the old woman is taken to a hospital. Emily goes through the old woman's bags and suddenly feels a rush of sympathy. She hurries to the hospital where she communicates her new-found sympathy. Excellent for raising the viewer's consciousness of others' problems.

Film Rental Center of Syracuse University
1455 East Colvin Street
Syracuse, NY 13210

The Therapeutic Community
28 minutes, color, rental fee: $15.00

The remarkable story of the transformation of a traditional mental hospital geriatric ward into a dynamic therapeutic community. Elderly patients, many of them long-term residents of the hospital, gradually take charge of their lives, through participation in a planned rehabilitation program. The film offers an optimistic, effective, and practical approach to treatment for elderly residents of institutions.

University of Michigan
Audiovisual Education Center
416 Fourth Street
Ann Arbor, MI 48109

Taking Care of Mother Baldwin
20 minutes, black & white, rental fee: $15.00

Old black woman and young black boy help each other cope. Film explores the relationships between the old, the young, and the work that must be done.

Film Rental Center of Syracuse University
1455 East Colvin Street
Syracuse, NY 13210

Weekend

12 minutes, color, rental fee: $15.00

This brief moving film depicts the plight of an old man being put gently out to pasture by his family. In the course of a normal family picnic in the countryside, it gradually becomes apparent that, for the grandfather, it is a one-way trip.

Mass Media Ministries
2116 North Charles Street
Baltimore, MD 21218

What Man Shall Live And Not See Death

57 minutes, color, rental fee: $20.00

This film examines attitudes and problems connected with the way western society has encouraged our dealing with death and bereavement. This is drawn from the research of Dr. Elisabeth Kübler-Ross and the experience of St. Christopher's Hospice for the terminally ill.

University of Illinois
Visual Aids Service
1325 South Oak Street
Champaign, IL 61820

University of Michigan
Audiovisual Education Center
416 Fourth Street
Ann Arbor, MI 48104

Ease On Down The Road

20 minutes, color, rental fee: $23.00

This film deals with the needs of the elderly and the ways in which some church and synagogue congregations have tried to respond to these needs. This is a motivational film, and much of its power lies in the comments and insights of the elderly themselves and in the attitude of church and synagogue members who work with older persons instead of "doing for" them. In all that it documents, the film points out that it takes just one person who cares to get things started.

TeleKETICS
1229 S. Santee Street
Los Angeles, CA 90015

When Parents Grow Old

15 minutes, color, rental fee: $25.00

From "I Never Sang For My Father" with Gene Hackman and

Melvyn Douglas. Theme: the problem of responsibility to the aging parents, and society's treatment of the elderly. A young man grapples with how to furnish care for his aging father.

Fortress Church Supply Stores Films Department
2900 Queen Lane
Philadelphia, PA 19129

The Wild Goose

19 minutes, black & white, rental fee: $40.00

A hilarious satiric comedy about a misanthropic old man confined in a straitlaced nursing facility. The puckish, fiercely independent oldster spends most of his time trying to circumvent the rules and regulations and the nurses who enforce them. His rebellion is complete when he contrives a wheelchair motorized, a la Rube Goldberg, by a power lawnmover. Disrupting the entire home, he makes a slap-stick escape.

Films Incorporated
440 Park Avenue South
New York, NY 10016

Replay

8 minutes, color, rental fee: $5.10

Provocative comment on the generation gap. This film compares the rather disdainful views toward current rock dancing, unconventional fashions, women's liberation, sex in the movies and fun with flashbacks of exhausting dance marathons, flapper fashions, early suffragettes, sultry silent screen stars, etc. Lyrical song comments on the fact that we're not so far apart—life is just a replay. Award winning.

University of Michigan
Audiovisual Education Center
416 Fourth Street
Ann Arbor, MI 48104

Elder Ed: The Wise Use Of Drugs

30 minutes, color

"Elder Ed" is an educational program in three parts, each of which includes a film portion designed to be followed by live discussion. Each deals with a particular aspect of drug use (prescription and over-the-counter). The three parts are titled

"Drug Problems, Communicating with Doctors"; "Buying Drugs Wisely"; and "Taking Drugs Carefully, Focusing on Healthy Aging."

Prevention Branch, National Institute on Drug Abuse
Room 10-A-30
Rockville, MD 20857

The Third Age: The New Generation

15 minutes, color, rental fee: $18.00

This film depicts the creative contribution older persons can and should give to society with the support of the church.

Audiovisual Library
The Christian Church (Disciples of Christ)
P.O. Box 1986
Indianapolis, IN 46206

Nell And Fred

29 minutes, black & white, rental fee: $7.80

This film documents the experience of an aged couple as they face an inevitable question: to move into a home for the aged where they can live and have medical attention, or to remain in their own home.

University of Michigan Audiovisual Education Center
416 Fourth Street
Ann Arbor, MI 48104

Everybody Rides the Carousel

A series of 3 films, 24 minutes each, color, rental fee: $30.00 each or 3 parts for $75.00

This film series is an animated view of the Stages of Life adapted from works of Erik H. Erikson. "Everybody Rides the Carousel" takes everybody along on the eight "rides" through the human life span, the eight stages of life described by psychologist Erikson. A profound and joyous excursion into the experience of life, each sequence unfolds the "pushes" and "pulls" of a cycle of human development.

Part I: Stage 1—The Newborn (trust/mistrust)
Stage 2—The Toddler (autonomy/shame and doubt)
Stage 3—Childhood (initiative/guilt)

Part II: Stage 4—School (competence/inferiority)
Stage 5—Adolescence (search for identity—leader/dreamer)

Stage 6—Young Adulthood (intimacy, love, friendship/ loneliness, isolation)

Part III: Stage 7—Adulthood (caring for the next generation/ stagnation)

Stage 8—Old Age (acceptance of death, integrity/despair)

Begin With Goodbye

A series of 6 films, 28 minutes each, color, rental fee: $35.00 each or 6 parts for $180.00

These six films explore changes involving work, relationships, body change, the loss of loved ones and our own death. The six films are as follows:

"Changes" introduces the theme of the series—that all of life is beginnings and endings, each involving saying goodbye to yesterday so we can get on with tomorrow.

"Mirror, Mirror on the Wall" treats the seldom-discussed topic of physical loss, bodily changes, which involve not merely our vanity, but our very identity. Quinby Schulman, who recently underwent a radical mastectomy, and Island Matthews, who experienced a heart attack, are interviewed.

"Exits and Entrances" deals with personal relationships which endlessly come into being or cease to be. Personal profiles include Deborah Wade, a Native American woman who leaves home to attend nursing school on a large and impersonal campus, and a family facing the trauma of divorce.

"Turned Loose" focuses on changes related to our work. The segment includes interviews with Al Durham, who has been laid off his construction job, and John Suzuki, a research scientist who recently retired.

"A Time To Cry" explores the loss of a loved one. Harriet Kerr recalls the death of her husband and her struggle to begin a new life as a widow. Sandy and Bob Spencer attempt to prepare themselves and their childen for Sandy's impending death as a victim of cancer.

"The Death of Ivan Ilych" introduces the most profound change any of us can imagine—our own death. A dramatization of Tolstoy's moving short story is performed for a group of seriously ill hospital patients who afterward share their responses, each person recognizing some aspect of his or her condition in the Tolstoy story.

Mass Media Ministries
2116 North Charles Street
Baltimore, MD 21218

C. Organizations in Field of Aging

1. Canada

Canadian Association on Gerontology
c/oDepartment of Psychology
University of Calgary
Calgary, Alberta
Canada T2N 1N4

The Canadian Council on Social Development
Box 3505 Station C.,
Ottawa, Ontario
Canada K1Y 4G1

National Pensioners Concerned (Canada), Inc.
51 Bond Street
Toronto, Ontario
Canada M5B 1X1

National Pensioners and Senior Citizens Federation
3505 Lake Shore Boulevard West
Toronto, Ontario
Canada M8W 1N5

Pensioners Concerned (Canada), Inc.
51 Bond Street
Toronto, Ontario
Canada M5B 1X1

2. United States

American Association of Homes of the Aging (AAHA)
1050 17th Street, N.W.
Washington, DC 20036

Represents nonprofit homes for the aging—religious, municipal, trust, fraternal. Provides a unified means of identifying and solving common problems to protect and advance the interests of the residents served. Relates to government agencies, has several publications, and sponsors an annual convention.

National Retired Teachers Association/American Association of Retired Persons (NRTA/AARP)
1909 K Street, N.W.
Washington, DC 20049

Has a membership of several million persons 55 years of age or older, both retired and not retired. The aim is to enhance every aspect of the lives of older people. Publishes AARP's *Modern Maturity,* NRTA's *Journal,* and *Dynamic Maturity* (actually produced by Action for Independent Maturity, a division of AARP for persons 50 years of age). Has programs for retirement planning, insurance, and prescription drugs.

American Nursing Home Association (ANHA)
(American Health Care Association)
1025 Connecticut Avenue, N.W.
Washington, DC 20036

A federation of state associations of nursing homes, it includes profit and nonprofit homes. Prepares an annual compilation of nursing home and bed totals and welfare payments by state. In addition to a 2,000-volume library, ANHA has several publications.

American Public Welfare Association (APWA)
1313 East 50th Street
Chicago, IL 60637

Has prepared teaching materials in anticipation of the spread of gerontological training through universities and professional schools.

The Gerontological Society
One Dupont Circle
Washington, DC 20036

A professional society, promotes scientific study of the aging process, publishes information and important periodicals, and holds a national meeting annually and an international meeting every three years.

Gray Panthers
3700 Chestnut Street
Philadelphia, PA 19104

An activist group fighting against stereotyping and injustice regarding older people.

The National Caucus on the Black Aged
1730 M. Street, N.W., Suite 811
Washington, DC 20036

Works for improving quality of life of the black aged. Relates to the National Center on Black Aged (Same address), which provides coordination, information, and consultative services to meet their needs.

National Council of Senior Citizens(NCSC)
1511 K Street, N.W.
Washington, DC 20005

With membership of all ages, represents and lobbies for needs of the elderly.

National Council on the Aging (NCOA)
1828 L Street, N.W. Suite 504
Washington, DC 20036

A voluntary agency, provides leadership services for organizations and individuals concerned with aging. Sponsors the National Institute on Senior Centers, the National Institute on Industrial Gerontology, and National Voluntary Organizatons for Independent Living for the Elderly. NCOA has many publications and holds annual national and regional conferences.

National Interfaith Coalition on Aging (NICA)
298 S. Hull Street
(P. O. Box 1924)
Athens, GA 30605

An instrument for cooperative effort by religious organizations to sensitize churches and synagogues to their responsiblities in improving the life of older adults. Holds annual conferences and conducts special projects. The Lutheran Church in America is an active member.

D. Government Agencies in Field of Aging

1. Canada

a. National

Department of National Health and Welfare
Income Security Programs Branch
(Old Age Security, Guaranteed Income Supplement, and Spouse's Allowance)
Ottawa, Ontario
Canada K1A 0L4

There are regional offices in all provinces. The Yukon and Northwest Territories are covered by the Edmonton, Alberta office.

New Horizons
Department of National Health and Welfare
Ottawa, Ontario
Canada K1A 1B0

There are regional offices in all provinces; the Yukon and Northwest Territories are covered by the Alberta office.

Policy Research and Long-Range Planning Branch (Welfare)
Miss Lola Wilson, Consultant on Aging
Ottawa, Ontario
Canada K1A 0K9

Canada Pension Plan
Tower "A" Place Vanier
333 River Road
Ottawa, Ontario
Canada K1A 0L1

There are district offices in various locations in all provinces and territories.

Quebec Pension Board
(Quebec Pension Plan)
P.O. Box 5200
Quebec City, Quebec
Canada G1K 7S9

b. Provincial

For the address of your provincial office with responsibility for aging inquire of your legislative representative, one of your local offices in charge of public services, or of one of the federal agencies listed.

2. United States

a. National

Administration on Aging (AoA)
Department of Health and Human Services
Office of Human Development
330 C Street, S.W. (HHS South)
Washington, DC 20201
(202) 245-0724

Write to the Administration on Aging for an up-to-date list of the ten federal regional offices, which handle much of AoA's work. Publishes *Aging*—$4.85 per year.

House of Representatives
Select Committee on Aging
Room 712 House Office Building, Annex 1
300 New Jersey Avenue., S.E.
Washington, DC 20515
(202) 225- 9375
Write for the Committee's newsletter, *News*

Senate Special Committee on Aging
G-225, Senate Office Building
Washington, DC 20510
(202) 225-5364
Write for Committee's newsletter, *Memorandum.*

Social Security Administration
Department of Health and Human Services
6401 Security Boulevard
Baltimore, MD 21235

b. State

For the address of your state office on aging contact your Area Agency on Aging (AAA), one of your state legislators, or the U.S. Administration on Aging at the above address.

c. Local

For information about local services, check with your city or county government (there may be an office on aging) or with the nearest Social Security office (listed in telephone directory under U.S. Government).

Index